MASTER CLASS

DJ Techniques
Vinyl and Digital

by CHARLIE SPUTNIK
Edited by Donny Gruendler

All Music Composed and Programmed by
Charlie Sputnik and Friends
Video Production by
Jon Hastings, Donny Gruendler, and Jace McDonald at Inc. Studios
Videography by
Jon Hastings, Paper Submarine
Audio Mixing and Mastering by
Donny Gruendler

To access video visit:
www.halleonard.com/mylibrary

Enter Code
7301-5274-0585-2689

ISBN: 978-1-4803-9372-1

Visit Hal Leonard Online at
www.halleonard.com

Contact Us:
Hal Leonard
7777 West Bluemound Road
Milwaukee, WI 53213
Email: info@halleonard.com

In Europe contact:
Hal Leonard Europe Limited
Distribution Centre, Newmarket Road
Bury St Edmunds, Suffolk, IP33 3YB
Email: info@halleonardeurope.com

In Australia contact:
Hal Leonard Australia Pty. Ltd.
4 Lentara Court
Cheltenham, Victoria, 3192 Australia
Email: info@halleonard.com.au

Contents

Preface

After studying classical piano in my early years, my background as a musician was originally established in punk and indie rock. I played in many bands as a vocalist, songwriter, and guitar player. I became interested in electronic music around the mid 1990s and started writing, recording, and releasing electronic music records in the late 1990s.

Well Roundedness

Because I have always been a multi-instrumentalist, interested in many instruments and genres of music, it appeared essential to me to be able to navigate many different styles of music. Among my many musical experiences, I have produced a hip-hop album with teenagers from what was then known as South Central LA, played guitar in jazz combos from Boston to Las Vegas, rocked CBGB in New York City with French punk bands, and DJ'd all over the world, from cafés in Helsinki to Brazilian beaches.

To this day, I not only DJ, but write, compose, produce, arrange, and perform in a wide array of projects, including advertisements, radio jingles, movie trailers, remixes, etc. I also produce music events at film festivals, fundraisers, and corporate parties, sometimes paired with dancers, performance artists, videographers, etc. I have never stopped performing live, whether solo or with various bands.

Education and Key Encounters

Right as I was studying jazz at Berklee College of Music, a fine establishment I would graduate from in 2000, I met an individual who would become a very important person in my life, as well as my main musical partner for years to come: Arthur Pochon, AKA Art Bleek. Art was a saxophone- and piano-playing prodigy when I met him, and he was just starting to dabble with electronic music production when we met. A classically trained musician, he reinforced my belief that it was possible to create music in all kinds of genres and that one didn't need to remain focused on a single style to blossom creatively.

Art and I began working together in 1997 and have since then recorded hundreds upon hundreds of tracks in many styles, including jazz, electro-swing, house music, R&B, French Chanson, hip-hop, techno, down tempo, reggae, indie pop, etc.

Becoming a DJ

Upon moving to Los Angeles, I was offered an opportunity to become a resident DJ in a brand new, upscale lounge in West Hollywood. I believe I was hired because they were looking for a very eclectic DJ, who could switch from J.S. Bach's Goldberg Variations to Miles Davis' Live-Evil without blinking.

Although I had released vinyl records in England with Art Bleek, I was not yet a DJ at that time. I spent the summer before the club opened studying beat matching on vinyl with my close friend DJ Erwan, who had been a resident in top Australian and Eastern European clubs and had opened for Carl Cox.

This initial residency led to many opportunities, including DJing movie premieres for Warner Bros., Universal, Sony Pictures, and Disney among others, as well as landing high profile gigs such as playing with a traditional Taiko drumming ensemble from Japan and a fifty-piece orchestra for the official inauguration of Los Angeles Airport's new international terminal.

Into the Future

My love of music and work as the Chair of the DJ Program at Hollywood's Musicians Institute led me to want to transmit and share knowledge about DJing to future generations.

This book, an introduction to the world of DJing, is by no means an exhaustive method covering all there is to know about DJing. Think of it instead as an overview of the main DJing techniques, from traditional vinyl to CDJs, to software-based solutions such as controllerism and Serato. I find that there is a certain mystery surrounding the DJ world, and it was especially interesting to uncover its secrets from the point of view of a musician.

As dematerialization of music continues, it is now possible to DJ directly using streaming services such as Spotify, and by using mobile devices such as tablets and mobile phones. This will certainly warrant the creation of a second book further exploring these exciting new technologies.

In the meantime, I sincerely hope you have as much fun reading this book as I have had writing it!

Sincerely,

Charlie Sputnik

Acknowledgements

My family and friends

First and foremost I'd like to thank my wonderful wife Anna-Tina Kessler for providing so much inspiration in my life; my partner in crime Arthur Pochon (Art Bleek), who has helped shape my musical personality over the years; my big brother and mentor Mark Bell (Blakkat), who trusted me enough to let me record with legends Chaka Khan and DJ Sneak among others; my German brothers Larse, Marco Niemerski (Tensnake), Adrian Hoffmann, and especially Manuel Tur, who has believed in me since the beginning; my London crew Chris Belsey and Jesse Rose from Loungin' Recordings, Trevor Loveys and Affie Yusuf from House of 909, Josh Harvey (Hervé) and Sinden (The Count and Sinden); Meik De Swaan and Christiaan Mcdonald from MusicMusic and Rush Hour in Amsterdam; Peter Wanders, Martin Kratzenstein, and Jurgen Kausemann at ChinChin records; my LA recording crew Damon Palermo (Magic Touch), Thibault Chabosson, and Erwan LeBayon; soul sista Novena Carmel; jazz heads Antoine Salem, Nick Rosen, Miguel Atwood-Ferguson, Michael Papillo, Jean-Paul Monsché, Robby Marshall, Lionel Loueke, and Ferenc Nemeth; Annabelle Pain; Stacey Esquith and Jessica Ripoll from Jordanah; Valida Carroll and Mathieu Schreyer from 89.9 KCRW; Martin Fleischmann from Rum N Humble; Anastacia McPherson; Catherine Goldwyn; Taka Boom; Chuck Hurewitz; my Austrian brothers Tommy Schobel and Boris Worister; electronic music pioneer Joachim Garraud; Annie Babin; master luthier James Trussart; JC Dhien; Sebastian Hinton; Yann Perreau.

This book would not have been possible without the support of class act Jace McDonald, Jon Hastings at Paper Submarine, and most particularly Donny Gruendler, whose confidence and guidance inspired the desire to create this book in the first place.

The fine companies that have supported me through the years

I would also like to thank the following music industry professionals who continue to support me to this day: Travis Kirschbaum (TK Disco) at Beatport, Dave Hillel at Ableton, Sylvain Missemer at Arturia, Ryan Barnes and Keisuke Shingu at Pioneer DJ, Constantin Koehncke at Native Instruments, Jessica Sullivan at Avid, Matt Perry at Serato, Kathy Alexander at TC-Helicon, and Charles "Chuck" Ono at Stokyo.

About the Author

Video 1

Charlie Sputnik is a Los Angeles based DJ, vocalist, guitarist, and record producer. He is also:

- A Program Chair at Hollywood's Musicians Institute (M.I.).

- Currently collaborating with ten-time GRAMMY Award®-winner and legend Chaka Khan as a topline writer and vocalist on her next studio recording.

- A member of Zoowax, a project with gifted vocalist and funky princess Novena Carmel (Sly Stone's daughter) and Art Bleek. We play a mixture of house music and Dixieland jazz. Zoowax is signed on Germany's ChinChin Records and UK's Loungin' Recordings, available on CD, Spotify, and on iTunes.

- An artist that has performed live and/or DJ'd in various cities around the world such as LA, New York, Paris, London, Tokyo, Zürich, Cannes, Miami, Geneva, Helsinki, Rio de Janeiro, Hong Kong, Casablanca, etc. He has released broken beat and vocal house music on vinyl on prestigious labels such as True Romance (DE), Loungin' (UK), Good Mood Music (UK), Wagram (FR), Cheap Thrills (UK), and Sick Trumpet (UK), among others.

- A vocalist that has collaborated with musicians and producers Chaka Khan, Joachim Garraud, Groove Armada, DJ Sneak, Blakkat, Art Bleek, Manuel Tur, Trevor Loveys, Affie Yusuf, Larse, Magic Touch, Round Table Knights, and Hervé and Jesse Rose, to name a few.

- An alumnus (and graduate) of Boston's Berklee College of Music.

- A DJ that has spun at the official Hollywood premieres of movies such as 2012 Best Picture Academy Award winner *The Artist*, Clint Eastwood's *J. Edgar*, Steven Spielberg's *Lincoln*, and *The Adventures of Tintin* and *Blood Diamond*, among many others.

Charlie's list of corporate clients includes American Film Institute, Audi, American Airlines, Warner Bros., Universal Pictures, Sony Pictures, 20th Century Fox, E! Entertainment, Disney, Taschen, The French Consulate in Los Angeles, Westfield, University of Southern California, and Los Angeles World Airports among countless others. For more information, please visit charliesputnik.com.

Overview

Video 2

Explanation

This text is designed to help today's up-and-coming DJ become familiar with the main methods of DJing, understand the skills necessary to perform a convincing DJ set, and learn about the important historical and technological landmarks that have contributed to this art form. Not only will I present the traditional method of DJing using vinyl records, but I'll also share more modern methods of performance, including both digital media players (Pioneer CDJ/XDJs) and the industry-leading software Serato DJ as well. A later chapter on business will provide insightful advice gathered along years of experience, as well as useful tips and tricks for onstage performance. In addition to the above-mentioned step-by-step instructions, this package also includes online video mirroring all the concepts addressed in the book. Upon completing this study, the reader will be able to perform a convincing DJ set on a variety of DJ setups.

Basic musical assumptions

It is assumed that anyone reading this material has a basic knowledge of music and forms, including items such as: a verse and chorus, and bridge, as well as introductions, basic vamps, and outros. However, if you need any additional information on basic musical terminology or styles, there are many fine books available from Hal Leonard that can aid you in your studies.

What if you have never DJ'd before?

I certainly suggest that you find a reputable DJ instructor in your area and take some lessons to remedy the situation. However, I do realize that many of you reading this book do not have the resources to take lessons or do not have the time to attend those lessons. Therefore, you will have to intensify your conceptual and listening skills. This can be accomplished by viewing the accompanying video and by practicing the concepts presented until they are mastered.

Format: Order of study

Unlike many other instructional books, the topics presented in this book are not based on a series of incremental concepts or exercises. Rather, each unit (and corresponding track) presents material developed to be studied with a particular DJ setup in mind. Thus, it will be possible to practice on a variety of equipment and ultimately be comfortable using all major setup types.

For example:

- **Vinyl:** This traditional medium is currently experiencing a comeback and presents an unmatched experience (i.e. in terms of feel and enjoyment).

- **CDJ/XDJ:** Modern CDJ/XDJ players allow limitless track selection opportunities (via USB media) without the need for a computer onstage. This medium remains the club standard today, especially when DJing EDM or house music.

- **DJ Controllers:** These devices are affordable, versatile, and easy to use. As a result, controllers have made DJing significantly easier, and their popularity continues to grow.

$\quad \jmath = 102$

Tempo marking

In the video, you will hear me reference "bpm"; this moniker indicates that there are a certain number of beats per minute (bpm). In addition, this is usually related to a specific note value as well. So, the above example indicates that a quarter note equals 102 bpm. (This can also be written as: Quarter note = 102.)

Flyers

I have included many of my DJ performance flyers at the start of each unit. It is my hope that they will give you a glimpse into the world of the professional DJ and, most importantly, serve as inspiration as you work through each unit and subsequent module of study.

More than DJ'ing: It's time to talk about music

It is extremely important that you do not think *technically/gear-wise* when working through each unit, concept, or exercise. **This book is not only about DJ'ing alone; it is also about *music*.** Musical sophistication, beat matching, consistency, and comfort level take time to master. If you rush through the material and do not follow the proper methodologies—or read through each section of this text—you will be defeating the purpose of your study. Ultimately, a DJ is only as good as the tracks he/she chooses to play, and how and when these tracks are introduced and blended together.

Unit One: History and Equipment

Description

In this unit, you will learn about the historical significance of DJing and become familiar with the various components that comprise a DJ setup.

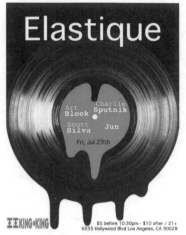

Upon completion of this unit, you should be able to:

- Understand the historical chronological order (and cultural significance) of DJing

- Name and install the various elements within a basic DJ setup

Module 1. Overview: A Brief History of DJing

The Early Days of Recorded Sound: The Phonautograph and Phonograph

Ex. 1

The earliest known recordings of sound date back to 1857, when Léon Scott invented the phonautograph (Ex. 1, left). It used a vibrating diaphragm and stylus to graphically record sound waves as tracings on sheets of paper. Although he had no intention of playing back any of these waves and was mainly interested in their visual analysis, the recordings of singing and speech, called phonautograms (recorded in 1860), were first played back in 2008.

In 1877, Thomas Edison invented the phonograph (Ex. 1.1), which, unlike the phonautograph, was able to both record and reproduce sound. After numerous experiments with wax-impregnated paper tape, Edison used tinfoil wrapped around a grooved metal cylinder and a stylus to record sound. This combination could play back sound immediately. Various versions of this device used tape and disc formats before Edison settled on a greatly improved version that employed a hollow wax cylinder. At the end of the 1880s, this wax phonograph cylinder helped to create the recorded sound market (record business). This format dominated the early years of the 20th century.

Ex. 1.1

Ex. 1.2

The Gramophone

In 1889, the first lateral-cut disc records were created by Emile Berliner, who named his system the gramophone. These records were first played with a small hand-propelled machine. In 1894, the 7-inch record appeared, along with a more substantial version of the gramophone. In 1901, 10-inch records were introduced, followed by the 12-inch in 1903.

In 1906, Reginald Fessenden successfully transmitted the first audio radio broadcast in history and played the very first record of a contralto singing Handel's *Largo* from *Xerxes*. In 1909, a sixteen-year-old named Ray Newby of Stockton, CA, began regularly playing records while attending Herrold College of Engineering and Wireless. He is considered to be the first radio disc jockey, or DJ. By 1910, radio broadcasting started to use live as well as pre-recorded sounds. In the 1920s, juke joints became popular places to drink and dance to recorded music played through jukeboxes.

Ex. 1.3

Although Edison continued to improve his cylinders, the basic patents for manufacturing lateral disc records expired in 1919, allowing other companies to start producing them. Analog disc records would remain the preferred way of playing back music for the foreseeable future (Ex. 1.3, left).

1930s–1950s: Disc Jockeys, Twin Turntables, and Sound Systems

In 1935, the term disc jockey was coined by radio commentator Walter Winchell, and first appeared in print in *Variety* in 1941. Martin Block's show, "Make Believe Ballroom," became an instant hit as he played records and created the illusion that he was broadcasting the nation's top dance bands performing live. At this time, the Federal Communications Commission favored live musicians, and it took a federal court ruling in 1940 to establish that a recording artist had no right to control the use of a record after it had been recorded.

In 1943, Jimmy Seville held the first DJ dance parties in London, and claimed that he was the first DJ to use twin turntables (for continuous play) in 1947. That year, the world's first discothèque, called the "Whiskey à Go-go," opened in Paris, France using recorded music instead of live musicians as the main entertainment.

In the Post-War era, the first DJ "stars" appeared on radio and were responsible for exposing the public to rock 'n' roll. DJ Alan Freed is often called the "father of rock 'n' roll" because he introduced this stylistic name on the radio. During the 1950s, sock hops and "platter parties" featured well-known radio DJs playing hits on single 45-RPM records. These DJs talked between songs and sometimes hired a live drummer to play beats between songs. In 1955, Bob Casey, a well-known sock hop DJ brought the two-turntable system to the US.

In the late 1950s, sound systems appeared in the ghettos of Kingston, Jamaica. Local DJs, called selectors, played dance music from large PA systems and created a style called "toasting" by chanting over the music in a rhythmic, boastful way.

1960s–1970s: Beat Matching and Modern Turntables

In the 1960s, nightclubs and discothèques gradually gained popularity over sock hops. This is when the first dedicated DJing systems appeared, notably Rudy Bozak's classic CMA-10-2DL mixer. In 1969, club DJ Francis Grasso popularized beat matching at New York's Sanctuary nightclub. Towards the end of the 1960s, neighborhood block parties modeled after Jamaican sound systems gained popularity in Europe and in the boroughs of New York City.

Ex. 1.4

In 1972, Technics released the first SL-1200 turntable shown in Ex. 1.4 (left), which remains an industry standard to this day. During the 1970s, hip-hop music and culture began to emerge within New York City's African American and Latino youth. The four main elements of hip-hop culture are: graffiti, breakdancing, MCing (rapping), and DJing.

In 1973, Jamaican-born DJ Kool Herc (Ex. 1.5), widely regarded as a "founding father of hip-hop," performed at block parties in the Bronx and developed a technique of mixing back and forth between two identical records to extend the rhythmical instrumental segment, or break. Turntablism, the art of using turntables not only to play music, but also to manipulate sound and create original music, began to develop.

Ex. 1.5

In the mid 1970s, a soul-funk blend of dance pop known as disco emerged in the mainstream music charts in the US and Europe, causing discothèques to experience a rebirth after a relative decline towards the end of the 1960s. The DJ's record collection became the sole source of entertainment, thus differentiating themselves from earlier clubs, which featured live bands. In 1975, the concept of record pools emerged, allowing DJs to receive the newest music from the recording industry in an efficient method.

In 1975, hip-hop DJ Grand Wizard Theodore invented the scratching technique by accident. In 1979, Sugar Hill Gang released "Rapper's Delight," the first hip-hop record to become a hit. This record introduced the technique of sampling to the masses, since it used the bass line from the song "Good Times" from the group Chic.

1980s

In 1981, the cable TV network MTV was launched and was exclusively devoted to playing music videos. The studio talent who introduced each of the videos became known as the "VJ" or video jockey. In 1982, "Planet Rock" by Afrika Bambaataa (Ex. 1.6) was the first hip-hop song to feature synthesizers, heavily influenced by German electronic music pioneers Kraftwerk. In 1982, the compact disc (CD) was introduced, the first mass market digital medium for entertainment. The arrival of the CD is often seen as making today's digital audio revolution possible.

In the early 1980s, Larry Levan, a NYC disco DJ, gained cult status thanks to his eclectic mixes. He was responsible for inspiring a new type of music called garage. At the same time, in Chicago, a disco-influenced style of dance music called house music emerged, which was essentially disco music with added electronic drum machine beats and a synth bass line.

Ex. 1.6

In Detroit, techno music was in its infancy and differentiated itself from its disco roots by relying solely on electronic sounds.

In 1986, "Walk This Way," a collaboration between Aerosmith and Run DMC, became the first hip-hop song to reach the Top 10 on the Billboard Hot 100.

1990s

During the early 1990s, the rave scene, accompanied by savvy marketing, established the first superstar DJs, allowing them to create marketable brands around their names and sound. The CD began to take over as the medium of choice for club DJs, but vinyl records continued to remain popular in hip-hop circles, despite a decrease in production. By the end of the 1990s, trance music emerged from the German underground and quickly became one of the most dominant forms of dance music thanks to its repetitive, hypnotic sound.

In the late 1990s, the MPEG and the MP3 emerged as file formats aimed to reproduce acceptable sound quality at low bit rates, ultimately eliminating the constraints of traditional physical media. As a lossless compression scheme, the MP3 revolutionized the digital music domain and led to the creation of Napster, the first of the hugely popular peer-to-peer file sharing systems.

In 1998, the first MP3 digital audio player was introduced, later perfected to massive commercial success by Apple with its iPod (Ex. 1.7). The first digital DJ system allowing manipulation of MP3 files through special time-coded vinyl or CDs appeared with FinalScratch, a product developed by Stanton and Dutch company N2IT, and later by Native Instruments. While die-hard vinyl DJs remained reluctant to use these new tools, it soon became clear that this emerging technology was here to stay.

Ex. 1.7

2000s–Today

The most significant development in the way music is consumed today has been the rapid growth of streaming. Ubiquitous, fast, and always-on Internet access has allowed new platforms such as Spotify and Apple Music to emerge as dominant players in this quickly expanding new market. New generations of music lovers no longer find it necessary to acquire physical or digital copies of the songs they like since they can now stream an unlimited amount of music via their Internet-enabled devices. Fast connection speeds ensure immediate access to high-resolution music delivered free of charge.

A few of the larger DJ hardware manufacturers reacted to this change in music distribution and consumption by introducing new DJ controllers able to stream music wirelessly. For example, the Numark iDJ Pro (Ex. 1.8) allows DJs to mix tracks directly from Spotify. Although this segment will likely grow quickly in the future, most DJs are uncomfortable about relying on sometimes unpredictable WiFi connections, and still prefer mixing with digital copies of their tracks, located on their machines' hard drives or on an external drive.

Ex. 1.8

Some new DJ controllers bypass the computer or the tablet altogether. Large multi-color display screens on the controllers themselves coupled with ever expanding portable USB storage solutions remove the need for a laptop. Pioneer's XDJ-RX2 all-in-one controller (Ex. 1.9) is one of these systems.

Ex. 1.9

Module 2. The Basic DJ Setup: Presentation and Installation

Video 5

In spite of the progress made by digital platforms, traditional vinyl turntables and CD turntables remain very prevalent. Therefore, it is important for aspiring DJs to understand the various elements that make up each setup.

You will need the following elements:

- 2 vinyl turntables
- 2 cartridges (also referred to as "needles")
- DJ mixer
- Slipmats (felt mats that go between the record and the turntable platter)
- DJ headphones
- Vinyl records
- 2 RCA cables

Vinyl Turntables

Vinyl turntables are the hallmark of any traditional DJ setup. Just like any other instrument, each DJ will have a certain preference of model and/or feature set. However (and at the time of this publication), the industry-standard turntable is the Technics SL-1200 MK2.

Technics SL-1200 MK2

Ex. 1.10

The new SL-1200 MK2 (Ex. 1.10) has become a near-mythical piece of machinery. The hip-hop community calls it the "Wheel of Steel" and uses it to create the signature sound of hip-hop: "the scratch." Only the SL-1200 MK2 has a motor capable of continually withstanding the abuses of record-gripping stops and high torque starts that comprise hip-hop's infamous scratch technique. Although all Technics SL-1200 models have been discontinued, they remain the vinyl turntable industry standard and can still be found in many clubs around the world.

Numark TT250USB

The Numark TT250USB turntable is actually preferred by some DJs to the Technics SL-1200. It features a USB connection for easy vinyl-to-digital file conversion. It has a lot of torque (the "spinning power" of the platter) and it is fully adjustable. The increased torque significantly reduces the start and stop times of the record. Also, the TT250USB features a 1/8-inch input connection so that mixers with remote start capability can control the unit by raising a fader.

Ex. 1.11

Stanton STR8-150

The Stanton STR8-150 has the ability to play 33-, 45-, and 78-RPM records. It also features an S/PDIF digital output so that the turntable can be plugged into a computer's sound card or a digital surround receiver. This Stanton model comes standard with a good DJ cartridge, which most other turntables do not. One drawback however, revealed in benchmark tests, is its relatively high wow and flutter, clocking in at 0.1. In comparison, the Technics models boast wow and flutter of 0.01.

Ex. 1.12

Reloop RP-8000

The unit is able to communicate directly with DVS software via USB, including Serato DJ, making boxes and a Serato-enabled mixer unnecessary. It also features eight performance pads allowing cue, sampler, loop, and slicer control directly from the unit. A bpm counter makes beat matching even easier, and a high-resolution pitch control of +/- 50% can be shown on the LCD display. Up to four turntables can be linked via USB.

Ex. 1.13

Cartridges

Turntable cartridges are one of the most important parts of a DJ setup as they (along with the tonearm) read the vibrations of a record's groove. These vibrations are picked up by the needle (also called a stylus) and are transferred to the cartridge. Good cartridges, combined with a good stylus, will reproduce minute details of a recording. Good cartridges will exhibit close to a "linear frequency response," whereby the lowest to the highest notes are played at very close to the same volume. Inferior cartridges often have "spikes" where the music becomes louder at a particular frequency. Let's take a look at a few popular models.

Shure V15

One of the storied cartridges is the Shure V15. Developed in a time when the Shure brand did not face any substantial competition in this segment, the Shure V15 established a quality standard that all other manufacturers could measure against. Although the V15s were discontinued in the late '90s, they can still be found secondhand for several hundred dollars.

Ex. 1.14

Shure M44-7

Along with the V15, Shure released the M44-7 and the M44-G cartridges. These models have legendary tracking ability and have been used by battle DJs since the early days of turntablism because of their ability to track to any record, warped or not. The M44-7's bass response is extremely weighty and pronounced, which makes it a favorite of hip-hop DJs, while the M44-G has warmer trebles and lighter bass.

Other cartridges of note are the Audio Technica AT440MLb, the Ortofon Concorde, and the Stanton GrooveMaster V3.

Ex. 1.16 (below)

Ex. 1.15

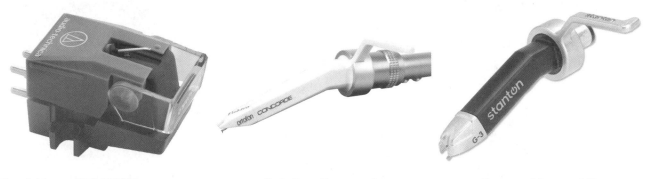

Ex. 1.16   AT440MLb   Ortofon Concorde   GrooveMaster V3

DJ Mixers

The key features differentiating a DJ mixer from a regular mixer are the ability to redirect (cue) a non-playing source to the headphones as well as the presence of a cross fader, which allows for an easier transition between two sources.

A DJ mixer usually has from two to six stereo channels. Channels can usually accommodate phono inputs for turntables and line inputs for sources such as CD players. Each individual channel features an equalization section used to fade parts of the track in and out. Advanced mixers feature built-in effects. Cue switches send out the signal to the headphones, allowing the DJ to preview and beat match a track without sending it to the master output. Simple mixers have two channels and a cross fader, sometimes with a button reversing the cross fader's direction. More advanced mixers have assignable cross faders in which each channel can be assigned to either end of the cross fader or bypass the cross fader entirely. Many scratch mixers have a cross fader curve control that changes the distance the cross fader needs to travel to fully open the channel, which is useful for speedy scratching. Additionally, one or two mic inputs may be present to accommodate MCs.

Popular DJ Mixers

Rane's TTM57MK2

This Rane mixer has become hugely popular because it offers a built-in connection to the Serato DJ software. It features two USB ports for seamless DJ changeover, ten record and ten playback channels per port, sample rates of up to 96 kHz, and dedicated effects by iZotope for each deck, and three high- and low-pass sweep filters. Also, it doesn't require drivers on a Mac.

Ex. 1.17

Pioneer DJM-900NXS2

This mixer features Pioneer's first ever 64-bit mixing processor for a warmer, more nuanced sound along with fine-tuned EQ, fader curves, and six studio-quality sound FX. It also has an independent Send/Return, four phone inputs, and two USB ports. It allows quick access and manipulation of the parameters of each beat effect with its X-Pad controller. It features fully assignable MIDI controls, XLR/RCA outputs, 1/4 TRS jack booth, RCA Rec, and digital coaxial outputs. It is fully compatible with Serato DJ and Traktor Pro software.

Ex. 1.18

Denon DN-X1800 PRIME

It features four phono/line inputs, dual USB ports, adjustable EQs, and a high-performance 24-bit/96-kHz sound card. Each channel features high quality Sweep FX as well as a dedicated filter knob. It also has an additional BPM FX panel with 14 extra effects. It features MIDI out ports for drum machines, instruments, and effects boxes.

Slipmats

A slipmat is a circular piece of cloth or synthetic material placed on, or instead of, the traditional rubber mat. Unlike the rubber mat, which is made to hold the record in place, the slipmat is designed to slip on the platter, allowing DJs to manipulate a record while the platter continues to rotate underneath. This is useful for holding the record still for slip-cueing, making minute adjustments during beat matching, and mixing and pulling the record back and forth while scratching.

Ex. 1.19

Ex. 1.20. A Felt Slipmat

Headphones

True DJ headphones have to reproduce accurate sound from the mixer, isolated from crowd noise, and be sturdy enough to withstand travel and abuse. They usually feature at least one rotating, reversible ear cup so the DJ can easily beat match the track currently playing on the sound system with the upcoming track before he mixes it in. Finally, they usually connect through a single cable coming from one ear cup in order to minimize cable dangling.

Ex. 1.21. Sennheiser HD8 DJ Headphones with Swivel Ear Cups

Understanding the Basic CD Setup

The CD turntable setup is most popular among club DJs because it offers more control and features than a vinyl setup. CD turntables with USB inputs can play digital files from thumb drives as well as hard drives. Custom CDs can be used, and most CD turntables can play MP3 CDs as well. Also, CD turntables do not require cartridges or slipmats.

You will need the following elements:

- 2 CD turntables
- DJ mixer
- DJ headphones
- CDs or MP3s
- 2 RCA cables

Compact Disc Turntables

Denon DJ SC5000 Prime

This multi-media player from Denon is the first of its kind capable of on-board music file analysis. It features three USB and one SD inputs for music playback, and its LAN outputs can connect up to four players. It has a 7-inch HD display with multi-touch gestures, 24-bit/96 kHz digital audio outputs, eight multifunction trigger pads for Cues, Loops, Slices, and Rolls, and plays all uncompressed and compressed audio formats, such as FLAC, ALAC, and WAV.

Ex. 1.22

Pioneer CDJ-2000 NXS2

This flagship media player from Pioneer DJ features WiFI connection, iPhone/Android connectivity, and SD and USB ports found in its predecessor the CDJ-2000 NXS, but adds a larger, multicolor touch screen with a Qwerty keyboard and search filters to help select tracks faster. It also has two banks of four Hot Cues and a high-end 24-bit/96 kHz digital sound card. Its ProDJ Link feature enables up to four players or laptops via a LAN connection, and its 7-inch full-color touch screen provides direct access to important features such as Wave Zoom, Needle Countdown, Phases Meter, and more.

Ex. 1.23

Installation

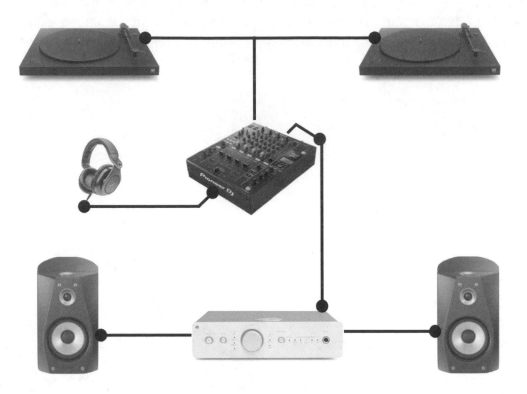

Ex. 1.24

Start by making sure that all the elements are laid on a sturdy, flat, and stable surface and that no cables are tangled under the feet of the turntables or under the mixer.

With a vinyl setup, always ensure you plug the RCA cables from the turntables into the "phono" input of the mixer, matching colors accordingly. When using CD turntables, connect through the "line" input.

Connect the ground wire from the turntables to the mixer. The appropriate connecting spot will usually be a twistable knob that the flat metal U-shaped cable tip can slide under. Once the tip is in place, tighten the knob, securing the cable firmly into place. Make sure you do this for both turntables. Grounding is important to prevent feedback, distortion, or other interference that the turntables can pick up if not correctly grounded.

Once all the elements are installed and powered off, make sure that all gains and volume controls are set to zero on the mixer. This prevents potentially damaging voltage surges from reaching the mixer's inputs.

Video 6

With a vinyl setup, it's important to balance your needles for proper operation. This step will ensure that there is adequate pressure on the record to prevent skipping, but not so much as to cause excessive wear on the needle or on the record itself. Adjust the cylinder weight on the back of the tone arm until the arm floats in the center, not tipping to either side, then roll on about three grams of pressure using the gauge on the weight.

Ex. 1.25

Power on the turntable and the mixer, put a record on, and press Play. Gradually increase the level on the mixer's channel until the meters are just below the red. Do the same for the other turntable.

Once the gain levels are set, increase the master volume to an adequate level. Don't turn the master volume all the way or the music might distort. Set it to about 50% and adjust the volume on the PA system or the headphones level. This will leave headroom on the mixer's volume, which will allow for easy adjustment during your set if needed.

Set the EQs to zero to prevent excessive coloration of the sound. Starting from neutral settings will allow you to hear the music as it has been recorded. You can then make adjustments as you see fit to harmonize the sound between various recordings, thus easing the transitions between them.

2 Unit Two: Optional Equipment and Introduction to Beat Matching

Description

In this unit, you will learn about optional equipment, effects units, and the main differences between vinyl and CD platforms. You will also learn about the basics of beat matching.

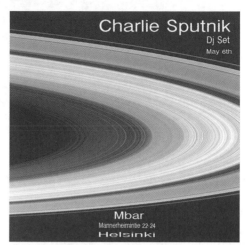

Charlie Sputnik
Dj Set
May 6th

Mbar
Mannerheimintie 22-24
Helsinki

Upon completion of this unit, you should:

- Be familiar with the optional pieces of equipment available to DJs

- Be familiar with the various types of effects units available

- Be able to compare vinyl and CD platforms

- Be able to comprehend the basics of beat matching

Module 1. Optional Equipment: Microphones and Effects Units

Ex. 2

Mics

Handheld microphones are useful for communicating with the audience, keeping the energy high on the dance floor, and introducing a new track or a new remix. A mic can also enable a guest MC or vocalist to rap or sing over a pre-recorded instrumental track. A handheld, dynamic microphone, such as the Shure SM58 (Ex. 2) is suited for live performance because of its durability and because it doesn't require "phantom" power (like condenser microphones). This type of microphone can be directly plugged into the DJ's mixer.

Mixers

Most DJ mixers feature at least one channel strip (Ex. 2.1) dedicated for a microphone input, with some mixers being able to accommodate two or more microphones. These channel strips often feature EQ control and can sometimes also be routed to the mixer's onboard effects, such as chorus, reverb, or delay. However, microphone channels on DJ mixers are meant to be used over instrumental tracks and rarely match the sound quality of a PA system and therefore, shouldn't be substituted for them.

Hardware Effect Units

Although the DJ world is shifting towards digital solutions, stand-alone hardware effect units are still attractive due to their analog grain and manu-facturing quality. Furthermore, some DJs prefer touching and operating a real fader or a real knob versus a computer mouse or trackpad. The Rodec Sherman Restyler, for example (Ex. 2.2), is great for creating classic low-pass, high-pass, or

Ex. 2.1

Ex. 2.2

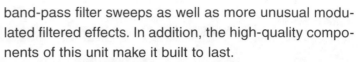

Ex. 2.3

band-pass filter sweeps as well as more unusual modulated filtered effects. In addition, the high-quality components of this unit make it built to last.

Korg Kaoss Pads have been embraced by DJs for many years. The KP3 unit (Ex. 2.3) presents an intuitive, powerful, and immediate control surface. It features 128 effects, such as vocoder, loopers, LFOs, EQs, Delays, etc. More than a simple effects processor, the KP3 is a complete instrument allowing performers to manage, recall, and play samples "on the fly," in addition to adding dynamic processing to any audio signal or to the samples themselves.

The Roland EF-303 (Ex. 2.4) is a stand-alone unit featuring numerous effects enabling DJs to take their performance a step further. Eleven of its effects can be synchronized to a BPM counter, and a turntable can be directly plugged into the unit. A 16-part step modulator has also been included, allowing construction of complex motion effect sequences. Finally, a monophonic synth controlled by the modulator provides the opportunity to write one's own bass lines in time with the records playing on the decks. A "grab" switch introduces effects that are rhythmically synchronized with the music.

Ex. 2.4

Module 2. Comparison of the Vinyl and CD Platforms

While most electronic musicians have made the switch from vinyl to CD turntables, die-hard hip-hop DJs continue to spin vinyl records. Here is an in-depth comparison of the two methods of traditional DJing:

Weight and Portability

Carrying records has long been a source of frustration, and their weight is one of the most important reasons a DJ chooses to go digital. A crate of vinyl records containing 80 to 100 records can weigh upwards of 50 pounds, whereas a similar number of CDs in a Case Logic CD book weighs less than 15 pounds.

Sound Quality

In many cases, the distinction between the two media boils down to personal preference. Vinyl uses a wider range of frequencies than CDs; however, the human ear cannot hear these additional frequencies. Vinyl is usually said to have a warmer, fuller sound, while CDs are said to have a thinner, digital sound. However, new advances in technology such as SACD or DVD-audio allow recordings to be encoded at a higher sampling rate as high as 24-bit and 96kHz, or even 192kHz before being sampled back down to the playback CD specification of 16-bit/44.1kHz. This allows for a far warmer sound reproduction, which is very reminiscent of analog recordings, even if the extra information might be inaudible to human ears.

Ease of Use in a Live Setting

The CD turntable (discussed in Unit 1) has become so sophisticated that it is virtually impossible to differentiate the scratching performed on these with scratching performed on traditional vinyl turntables. A traditional vinyl enthusiast might prefer the tactile sensation brought on by physically touching and manipulating the vinyl itself, i.e., placing a needle within the grooves and spinning the record backwards to find the first cue point. This technique is something that is only emulated on a CD player, not recreated. Indeed, although music on a CD can be manipulated via the large plastic platter controlling the CD player, the DJ isn't actually directly touching the medium on which the music is physically stored, but using a controller, a large joystick of sorts. That being said, CD players now come built with an array of effects and functions, such as on-the-fly looping.

Durability

Although CDs do wear out over the years and are vulnerable to scratches, vinyl records are much more fragile and require a lot of care. A CD can also store more music than a vinyl record, and can be duplicated countless times while retaining identical sound quality. Thanks to digital media in general, preserving music is easy, whereas once a rare vinyl record is damaged, it can be very difficult to replace.

Affordability

Apart from a few labels still pressing vinyl for a select audience of aficionados, the manufacturing cost of producing vinyl records is prohibitive resulting in new vinyl records becoming more and more rare. For this reason, music downloading (illegal or not) is seeing rapid growth, although pre-recorded CD sales are also dwindling. Thus, new vinyl production is quite small compared to that of these other two main music media.

Conclusion

As many venues do not provide specific equipment to a DJ, a professional should be comfortable using all types of DJ setups.

Module 3. Introduction to Beat Matching

Created in the late 1960s by DJ Francis Grasso, beat matching (sometimes known as beat mixing) is a basic DJing technique consisting of blending two records together by adjusting the speed of one record so that it matches the tempo of the other record. Grasso developed this technique in hopes of preventing people from leaving the dance floor between songs.

Once the two records are synced and the beats are occurring at the same time, it is then safe to transition from one record to another by seamlessly blending them together.

This basic technique of DJing ensures a smooth transition between songs without interruption in the music, thus helping the dance floor to remain full in a performance situation, such as playing in a club or at a party.

When done creatively, beat matching can result in unique remixes done "on the fly." For example, an instrumental version (or section) of a popular song can be played on record A while a well-known chorus from another song can be synced to it on record B. This skillful feat, while risky, can generate a huge response from a crowd.

Two songs that are relatively close in tempo with elements that complement each other can usually be beat matched by using the pitch control on one (or both) turntable(s).

Additionally, using the EQ controls on the mixer's strip will smooth the transition between records by ensuring that specific sound frequency ranges aren't muddied by too much information coming from both sources. For example, when relying on record A's four-on-the-floor kick drum to match and introduce record B, it is a good idea to turn record B's low frequencies all the way down on the mixer before gradually blending it in the mix. That way, there won't be two kick drums playing over each other. Finally, record A's kick drum can be gradually faded out while the low frequencies of record B can be turned up incrementally until record B's kick drum fully replaces record A's.

Modern mixers usually feature a digital BPM (beat per minute) counter, greatly easing the tempo adjustment process. Without this counter, DJs have to rely solely on their ear to determine if the record they are about to blend in needs to be accelerated or slowed down to match the tempo of the record that is still playing (i.e., on the spot live).

The process of learning to beat match can be frustrating and represents the toughest feat for a DJ. This skill separates experienced DJs from less-experienced ones. The time needed to master this technique differs from person to person and depends on one's natural musical ear. Patience is needed to hone this skill and requires a clear understanding of the task at hand.

3

Unit Three: Beat Matching and Mixing on Vinyl

Description

In this unit, you will learn about the historical significance of beat matching and become familiar with how to beat match on a traditional vinyl DJ setup.

Upon completion of this unit, you should be able to:

- Describe and identify beat matching techniques
- Beat match on a traditional vinyl turntable setup

Module 1. Learning to Beat Match Is Important

A DJ's ability to introduce a new track that matches the tempo of the current track is crucial. Not only does this technique minimize the disruption caused by the arrival of the new track, but also because it offers infinite creative possibilities. When faced with a "dance floor full" situation, there is a lot of pressure on the DJ to maintain the energy of the crowd. When the DJ successfully introduces a new track in a seamless manner, the crowd might not even notice that the song has changed because the beat hasn't stopped (and the tempo hasn't changed). In addition, beat matching provides the possibility of mixing an instrumental section of one song with a vocal section of another song, thus creating a never-heard-before mash up.

Beat matching on vinyl can be a perilous task because the DJ has to rely solely on his/her ears to identify whether the upcoming song's tempo is too fast or too slow. In comparison, a CDJ provides a digital beat counter, which indicates BPMs. With a beat counter, the DJ can adjust the new track to the tempo of the first track without having to rely on his/her ears to determine whether the track he/she is about to introduce is slower or faster. Software solutions such as Traktor or Serato DJ also feature BPM counters as well as graphics displaying the waveform of the audio files. The graphics allow the DJ to rely on visual aides to cue and beat match tracks. None of these features exist on a traditional turntable setup, which makes beat matching with real vinyl a challenge. It also requires a bit more practice.

However, BPM counters don't always work accurately, as some songs change tempos in the middle of the song. If you are playing a song that was recorded live at a show, for example, chances are the beat will slightly change and BPM counters will be completely useless. Similarly, a cappella tracks don't feature beats, which BPM counters need to determine a track's BPM.

There is a certain amount of prestige associated with being able to beat match solely on vinyl. Since a DJ never knows when he/she will be asked to DJ an "all-vinyl" set, having beat matching skills enables a DJ to jump on anyone's setup at any time, regardless of whether their setup is digital or not.

Knowing about BPM ranges of music will help you to find out how much songs can be sped up or slowed down before their sound quality starts to deteriorate. You will also be able to jump from one style to another without the crowd noticing. For example, you might be able to go from a house track to a chill out track just by halving the BPM of the house track. Similarly, you'll be able to go from dubstep to drum and bass by doubling the BPM of the dubstep track.

Listening to rhythms instead of looking at waveforms displayed on a screen will gradually teach you how music is constructed. One song might have a distinctive hi-hat, whereas another might have a recurrent synth stab or percussion loop you can latch onto. That way, your mixes will become a lot more intuitive and you will be able to jump from one style to another easily.

Beat matching by ear is one of the cornerstones of DJing. Once you have the basics covered, you will be able to take full advantage of all that digital systems have to offer. It is a process that is not easy, but is equivalent to "paying your dues." Plus, no one likes watching a DJ stare at a computer!

Tempo and BPM by Genre

In order to understand the relationship between BPM and genres, I have listed today's most popular styles alongside the appropriate tempos and playlist.

Disco (120 BPM)	Hip Hop (90–115 BPM)	Dubstep (approx. 140 BPM)
Abba - "Dancing Queen" Michael Jackson - "Don't Stop Til You Get Enough" Gloria Gaynor - "I Will Survive" Evelyn Champagne King - "Shame" Cheryl Lynn - "Gotta Be Real" Bee Gees - "Stayin' Alive" Shalamar - "Take That to the Bank" Sister Sledge - "We Are Family" Shannon - "Let the Music Play" Chic - "Le Freak"	The Message - "The Message" Dr. Dre - "Nuthin' but a 'G' Thang" Wu-Tang Clan - "C.R.E.A.M." Run DMC - "Run's House" Public Enemy - "Fight the Power" Sugarhill Gang - "Rapper's Delight" Grand Master Flash and the Furious Five - "Apache" Kendrick Lamar - "King Kunta" OutKast - "B.O.B." Eminem - "Stan"	Rusko - "Cockney Thug" Benga - "Flame" La Roux - "In for the Kill" (Skream Remix) Pinch - "Qawwali" The Bug - "Skeng" Mala - "Alicia" 12th Planet - "68" Coki - "Spongebob" LFO - "Kito"
House (120–135 BPM)	**Drum N' Bass (150–180 BPM)**	**Pop (110–140 BPM)**
Stardust - "Music Sounds Better with You" Daft Punk - "One More Time" Dennis Ferrer - "Hey Hey" DJ Sneak - "You Can't Hide from Your Bud" Eddie Amador - "Rise" François K - "Hypnodelic" Kerri Chandler - "On My Way" Frankie Knuckles - "The Whistle Song" Hardrive - "Deep Inside" Joe Claussell - "Je Ka Jo"	Roni Size - "Snap Shot" Rufige Kru - "Manslaughter" Goldie - "Inner City Life" Alex Reece - "Pulp Fiction" Bad Company - "The Nine" Adam F - "Circles" LTJ Bukem - "Horizons" Total Science - "Defcom 69" Camo & Krooked - "History of the Future" Underworld - "Skribble"	Madonna - "Like a Virgin" Wham - "Wake Me Up Before You Go-Go" Kylie Minogue - "Locomotion" Mariah Carey - "We Belong Together" Kim Carnes - "Bette Davis Eyes" The Police - "Every Breath You Take" Carly Rae Jepsen - "Call Me Maybe" Whitney Houston - "I Will Always Love You" Blondie - "Call Me" Ace of Base - "The Sign"

Techno 120–140 BPM
Kenny Larkin - "Clavia's North"
Random Noise Generation - "Hysteria"
Aqua Regia - "Pump Up the LEDs"
Aphex Twin - "Didgeridoo"
Ron Trent - "Altered States"
Basic Channel - "Octagon"
Millsart - "Steps to Enchantment"
Ben Klock - "Subzero"
Dave Clarke - "Wisdom to the Wise"
Kosmic Messenger - "Flash"

Module 2. Beat Matching on a Vinyl Setup

Accurately Counting BPM (Beats Per Minute) by Ear

Video 7

First, you must determine what type of vinyl record you are playing, which helps to set the turntable to the correct speed. On the Technics SL 1200 family of turntables, the RPM selector is below the spinning platter, to the left side of the turntable. If you are playing a 12-inch record, it is likely a 33 1/3 RPM record (although this is not always the case with EPs). However, if you are playing a 7-inch, it is almost guaranteed to be a 45 RPM record (very old 7-inch records were recorded at 78 RPM, but they are very rare nowadays).

Once you have set the correct type of record speed (otherwise usually indicated on the face of the record or on the record sleeve), you need to set the pitch control to exactly "0." On a Technics SL 1200 turntable, the pitch control fader is to the right of the vinyl platter. Dance music, such as house or techno, usually has "four-on-the-floor" bass drum kicks, which means that the kick drum will mark every beat. The number of kicks heard during a minute corresponds to the exact BPM count of the song. The easiest way to figure the BPM of a song is to count how many beats occur over exactly fifteen seconds and multiply that number by four, or do the same thing over thirty seconds and double that number. Knowing the BPM of a song will make things easier as it will allow choosing a song whose tempo is more or less similar to that of the first song.

One Simple Way of Beat Matching with Vinyl

Video 8

Mixing records is a skill that can take a long time to master. The following method is just one of many. A beginner should not become frustrated by the slow progress made, as learning to perfectly beat match can take months of practice:

1. Start playing a record on turntable 1 out loud.

2. Press the cue button on the mixer so you can hear turntable 2 in your headphones, but be sure that turntable 2's fader is turned down on the mixer.

3. Place the stylus at the beginning of the track on turntable 2.

4. Find the first beat, or cue point and hold the record while turntable 2's platter is spinning.

5. Release the record at the same time as one of the beats playing on turntable 1.

6. Chances are the new record will instantly sound like it's playing too fast or too slow.

7. Stop turntable 2's platter while turntable 1 is still playing out loud.

8. Adjust the pitch slider to the right of the platter on turntable 2. If the record introduced was too slow, then increase the speed by bringing the slider towards you; if it was too fast, reduce the speed by pushing the slider away from you.

9. Try finding the first beat again and release the record on turntable 2 one more time.

Video 9

10. Repeat steps 3–9 moving the pitch slider with smaller and smaller adjustments until the BPM of both records is roughly the same.

11. Although the two records are more or less beat matched, they will inevitably veer over time. To correct this, minute adjustments can be made: slightly pushing the label in the center of the record, or grabbing the center spindle and twisting it clockwise will accelerate the record, while lightly brushing one's finger against the platter will slow the track down. Fine tuning the tempo of records this way is known as pitch bending.

12. For more important adjustments, one can nudge the pitch control quickly back and forth, starting with large increments and "zeroing in" on the correct pitch in smaller increments. This technique is called "riding the pitch control."

Module 3. Bringing Up the New Track in Your Mix

Video 10

Now that the two tracks are more or less beat matched, it's time to bring up the new track in your mix. The method described below is ideal for a dancing club crowd. Obviously, if you are playing poolside in the afternoon, the quality of the transition might not be as crucial as when there are people dancing in front of you expecting the energy level to remain high in the club. In this case, there are several ways of bringing up the new track in the mix. The main goal is to make the introduc-

tion of the new song as seamless as possible, so it will be important to introduce the new track's various frequencies gradually as to not make the overall mix too muddy, too shrill, or simply overpowering.

One Simple Way of Bringing the New Record Up in the Mix

At this point, only the track playing on turntable 1 is playing out loud. Once the two tracks are properly beat matched however, you can gradually bring up the track playing on turntable 2 so that it can blend with the track playing on turntable 1.

The following is by no means the only method, but it works very well.

1. On the mixer, turn down the EQs for turntable 2's channel so that the frequencies of the new track don't interfere too much with the track playing on turntable 1.

2. Bring up the volume on turntable 2's fader to about two thirds.

3. Gradually swap the bass frequencies; meaning turn down the low end EQ on turntable 1's channel as you raise them on turntable 2's channel.

4. Raise the volume on turntable 2's channel to about 90%.

5. Gradually swap the EQs on the remaining frequencies (highs and mids).

6. Leave both tracks playing as long as possible.

7. When the tracks inevitably start to drift apart a bit, lower the fader for turntable 1.

That's it! You have successfully beat matched two tracks on vinyl!

Unit Four: Beat Matching and Mixing on CDJ

4

Description

In this unit, you will learn how to beat match on a CDJ setup. The similarities and differences between vinyl and CD approaches will also be presented in great detail.

DJ Fernando, DJ Dengue Feat. Charlie Sputnik
SATURDAY, AUGUST 21ST · PARADISE BEACH CLUB
TRANCOSO, BAHIA, BRASIL
NOON TILL SUNSET

Upon completion of this unit, you should be able to:

- Describe and identify beat matching techniques

- Beat match on a CDJ setup

Module 1. Beat Matching with CD vs. Vinyl

Both Technologies Have Their Advantages

Video 11

CD players were the first record-playing units to take advantage of today's near limitless digital technology. In addition to being easier to carry than vinyl records, CDs offer added capacity, especially if the tracks are encoded in a compressed format, such as MP3.

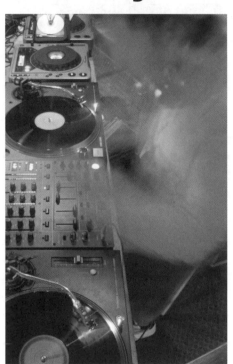

Vinyl records are exposed when used on turntables, which makes them more vulnerable to damage such as spilled drinks and various abuse. There is a much bigger chance for a vinyl record to become damaged while used in a club than a CD record. In addition, most CDs used today are burned CD-Rs, which are generally easy to replace.

Although scratching with a real vinyl is as close as the DJing experience gets, CD players are now extremely sophisticated and offer similar scratching capabilities, as well as countless looping (and sampling) possibilities. Provided the DJ is experienced, it is now virtually impossible to distinguish whether a record used for scratching is a vinyl or a CD.

Since observing the grooves on the record can give the DJ a fairly accurate estimate of the song's remaining time, vinyl records provide a visual and tactile experience. However, beat matching with CD players is generally considered easier than with vinyl turntables, for a variety of reasons:

Video 12

1. CD players generally feature BPM counters, which, while not infallible, provide good indications of the general tempo of the track.

2. Using the Jog/Dial wheel on a CD player generally provides a much more sensitive and precise experience than manipulating a piece of vinyl itself. The sole purpose of the Jog/Dial wheel is to be a controller: to adjust to the exact part of the song the DJ wishes to play. However, the vinyl IS the controller, in addition to being the medium on which the music is stored.

3. A CD player's Pitch Control fader can typically be assigned to cover a huge BPM range while a vinyl turntable's fader is usually limited to ±8% or sometimes ±16%, but rarely more. This makes switching from a very fast song to a very slow one theoretically possible, although this rarely sounds good in real life.

4. Finally, vinyl turntables don't have any kind of protection against skipping and can be at the mercy of loud bass frequencies causing the needle to jump. CD players typically have anti-skip features that prevent this from happening.

Module 2. Beat Matching on a CD Setup

Being Prepared

Video 13

Contrary to vinyl records, which usually feature the music of one group or artist (apart from compilation albums), the majority of the CDs used to DJ in clubs are homemade. It is crucial to carry a selection of fully encoded WAV/AIFF CDs even though they only contain 74 to 80 minutes of music. Although MP3 CDs can contain hundreds of songs each, the reality is that all clubs do not own CD players that can read MP3 CDs. Therefore, it is highly recommended to carry a selection of both. It is also recommended to listen carefully to each CD in its entirety to verify that no encoding errors happened during the burning process.

Video 14

One Simple Way of Beat Matching with CD Players

Video 15

Although CD players such as Technics CDJs offer a degree of control on the platter that is superior to that of a vinyl turntable, the basic skill of beat matching still presents a degree of difficulty and requires a lot of practice on a CD player.

1. Put a CD in CD player 1 and play it out loud.

2. Put a CD in CD player 2.

3. On CD player 2, find the first Cue point on the track by using the Seek buttons to find the very first beat.

4. Press the Play/Pause button as close to the ongoing beat as possible.

5. Use the Jog/Dial wheel on CD player 2 to locate the beat precisely. If your CD player offers a "Frame Searching" mode, place the start point just before the beat, as close as possible to it without actually hearing it.

6. Another way of doing this is to press the Cue button repeatedly to make sure the cue point is accurate enough. If it is, then the first beat should play exactly when the Cue button is pressed. Adjust this with the Seek button or the Jog/Dial wheel in cue-locating mode.

7. Start playing the track on CD player 2, and fast forward to the middle of the song using the Seek button. This is to find the maximum volume of the song.

8. Press the Cue buttons on the mixer to toggle between CD player 1 and CD player 2, and adjust the gain buttons to make sure the output levels of both channels are similar. This is to prevent one track from being much louder than the other.

9. Press the Cue button on CD player 2 to return to the cue point.

10. Press both Cue buttons on the mixer so you can audition both CD players.

11. While listening to the track played by CD player 1, press the Play button on CD player 2 exactly on the beat.

12. Chances are the new track will instantly sound like it's playing too fast or too slow.

13. Turn the side of CD player 2's Jog/Dial wheel to keep the tracks in sync. If you find that the new beat keeps falling behind, nudge the Jog/Dial clockwise. If it keeps speeding up, then nudge the Jog/Dial counter-clockwise.

14. If the new track keeps lagging and you have to keep pushing the side of the Jog Wheel clockwise, then adjust CD player 2's pitch slider by bringing it closer to you to speed the track up a little. On the other hand, if the new track is going too fast compared to the first one and you have to keep on nudging the Jog wheel counter-clockwise to slow it down, then push the pitch slider away from you to decrease the tempo.

15. Press the Cue button on CD player 2 again to return to the first cue point.

16. Repeat 11 to 14 until the tracks are beat matched and no further adjustments are needed. At this point, the tracks shouldn't veer off from one another; they should be staying perfectly beat matched over time.

17. Listen to the track playing on CD player 1 and find an appropriate spot to launch the new track.

18. Use the method described in unit 3's module 2 to bring up the new track in the mix.

That's it! You have successfully beat matched two tracks on CD players!

Module 3. Vinyl Mode vs. CDJ Mode

Video 16

Video 17

The latest CDJ players from Pioneer feature a switch that enables the player to be used in "CDJ" mode or in "Vinyl" mode. The main difference between these two modes is in the way the DJ is used to cueing up and stopping tracks.

Vinyl mode essentially enables the DJ to use the platter as if it were a vinyl turntable, allowing "scratching" and "cutting," which are essential tricks of the trade for a turntablist. Using the "Vinyl" mode is said to help DJs feel more connected to the record they are playing because it allows them to cue the tracks up manually, thus providing an experience that is closer to the one experienced on vinyl decks. However, "Vinyl" mode does create a risk of accidentally touching the platter and stopping the music!

CDJ mode will make the deck behave as a CD player. Pressing the Play/Pause button to pause playback will cause the deck to stop and begin repeating a small section of audio. This repeating section corresponds to the position where playback will resume when the Play/Pause button is pressed again.

CDJ mode will provide extra accuracy that is not possible in vinyl mode when cueing up tracks.

Here is a simple way to use a CDJ in "CDJ" mode:

If the cue point is placed right before the start of a beat, the stuttering heard when pressing "Cue" on the CD player is the very start of the attack of the beat, looped. Pressing the Play/Pause button exactly on the beat will release the new track with a lot of precision.

Video 18

While DJs coming from vinyl decks will often prefer "Vinyl" mode, it is important to know how to use CD decks in "CDJ" mode because only the newer and higher-end CD players provide "vinyl" mode. Also, a DJ never knows whether (or when) he/she will be asked to perform on an old Pioneer CDJ 200, which only provides a singular CDJ mode!

Module 4. First Song Analysis: Art Bleek— "Hecho en Pigalle"

Art Bleek—"Hecho En Pigalle"

French house music wizard Art Bleek has released over a hundred songs on dozens of prestigious labels. Although primarily known as a Deep House music producer, he uses his extensive musical training to produce records in all kinds of genres, including hip-hop, broken beat, electro-swing, jazz, etc.

"Hecho En Pigalle" is a good track to use for beat matching. It is based on a repeating melodic string motif, which is constantly yet slightly modified throughout the song. It also features breaks, risers, and sections that can be easily looped. This track being on the "harder" side of what Art Bleek usually produces, it matches the sobriety and intensity of the Jesse Rose track that will follow it.

Song Structure

0:00–0:22: Truncated string motif introduced, then bass line, then string pad idea

0:22–0.52: First drop of the main kick, string motif idea complete

0:52–1:52: Snare introduced after short "riser," beat reinforced, distinctive house sound with light snare and hi-hat

1:52–2:30: More "tribal" mini interlude

2:30–3:00: Kick reintroduced, full beat after short kick-less "riser"

3:00–3:22: Break: String idea modified and simplified

3:22–3:49: Beat reintroduced after short "riser"

3:49–4:15: Kick drops out, riser, hi-hat remains over string motif, then snare is reintroduced

4:15–5:15: Kick reintroduced

5:15–5:30: String motif shortened, then string pad reintroduced

5:30–5:52: Kick out for four bars, then reintroduced with string pad

5:52–End: Stripped down outro

Module 5. Second Song Analysis: Jesse Rose— "A-Sided"

Jesse Rose–"A-Sided"

Along with London DJs and producers Switch, Herve, and Trevor Loveys, Jesse Rose is credited with starting the "fidget house" sound. Jesse is the head of the Made to Play record label. After a stint in Berlin, Jesse has recently re-located to L.A.

"A-Sided" is a perfect track to beat match because it features clear sections, an infectious vocal loop intro and a huge bass motif dropped early on. Although simpler than Art Bleek's track, it also features a 45-second outro with no breaks, which is useful to set up the next song.

Song Structure

0:00 – 1:00: Sixteen bars of beats with no melodic elements, reinforced at 0:46 after a mini break

1:00: Main vocal loop introduced

1:30: Vocal loop 2 over a break

1:46: Main bass motif dropped, further developed at 2:25

2:46–3:06: 20-second break/interlude with no kick

3:06: 2nd drop with main vocal loop and bass motif reintroduced

3:36: Vocal loop reintroduced

3:46–4:06: 20-second break/interlude with no kick

4:06: Main musical idea reintroduced

4:50–End: Twenty-four bars of beats with no melodic elements

This song presents sections that can be looped effectively. This can help when concurrently introducing a new song, particularly the main vocal loop. A two-bar, four-bar, or eight-bar loop of this section can be used if using gear allowing on-the-fly loop creation; otherwise, the entire 30-second section essentially repeats the vocal motif over sixteen bars.

Module 6: One Way of Mixing the Two Songs

Using this main vocal section will allow easy beat matching because the vocal motif is very rhythmic, repetitive, and catchy. Effects such as phasing, delay, or pitch shifting can be applied to enhance the transition to another song.

Here is one way of mixing these two songs together. It is by no means the only way, but it does work quite effectively.

Let's start by cueing up "Hecho En Pigalle." If the song is playing at its original tempo of 128 BPM, then "A-Sided" will have to be slightly sped up using the pitch shift fader, since its original tempo is 127 BPM.

Let's let the track run until it's in full swing, so the crowd has a chance to appreciate the song.

Let's cue "A-Sided" on headphones and press play when "Hecho En Pigalle" is at 2:00.

Taking advantage of the beat staying steady on "Hecho," let's take a full minute to beat match it with "A-Sided."

In a perfect world, "A-Sided" should be beat matched by the time its main vocal motif arrives at 1:00. At this moment, "Hecho" is hitting its 3:00 break with a simplified string motif.

Blend both songs together by gradually inverting the EQ settings, lowering "Hecho"'s low-end while simultaneously raising "A-Sided"'s low-end. Turn down "Hecho"'s volume slightly and let "A-Sided"'s kick take the lead.

Listen in to "A-Sided," anticipating its drop, and when its bass motif drops at 1:46, turn "Hecho"'s volume down quickly and completely. At this point, "A-Sided" carries on by itself and it will soon be time to start looking for a new track to beat match it with.

This transition will be seamless as long as the DJ is very familiar with both tracks and is able to "feel" when "Hecho" gets lighter and provides a good opportunity for a blend, but more importantly to correctly anticipate the exact moment when "A-Sided"'s powerful drop appears.

5 Unit Five: Beat Matching and Mixing on CD

Description

In this unit, you will learn about beat matching two sets of specific songs. The use of EQ and filters will also be discussed.

Upon completion of this unit, you should be able to:

- Beat match two sets of specific songs, while employing the methods explained
- Utilize EQ and filters on a typical DJ mixer
- Understand the concept of equalization applied to DJing
- Understand the function of filters
- Enhance your mixing with the use of EQs and filters

Introduction to Set 1

Sometimes, during a set, there is a need to transition from one style of music to another. Maybe the club owner made it known that the style you are playing doesn't fit the venue, or the crowd is making you realize in no uncertain terms that they'd like to hear something else, or perhaps, there is simply a need for a change of pace. Whatever the reason, transitioning between styles of music can be tricky.

A crowd-pleasing way to successfully go from one style to another is to play a well-known song in the style you have been playing and beat match it with a song in a different style, but which features a sample from the first song.

This makes sense because, firstly, it should be easy to beat match the two songs since they feature the exact same sample, and secondly, because the crowd usually loves to hear music they already know. Also, although most people present should be familiar with at least one of the two songs, they should be thankful to be introduced to the song they don't know yet, but that carries a familiar element: either the song containing the original sample ("Aaah…THIS is where that sample came from!") or the newer song incorporating the original sample ("What a cool new way of using this classic sample!").

Either way, if the transition is done right, people might even forget that you radically changed styles!

Module 1. First Song Analysis: Lou Reed— "Walk on the Wild Side"

Lou Reed–"Walk on the Wild Side"

This song was the first solo hit for American musician Lou Reed, best known for his role as the leader of the 1960s cult group "The Velvet Underground."

Released in 1972 on Reed's second solo record *Transformer*, "Walk on the Wild Side" received wide radio coverage despite its content of taboo topics, such as trans-sexuality, drugs, and male prostitution.

The song, produced by David Bowie, is based on a plagal cadence, alternating from C to F. The F is played as a sixth chord. The pre-chorus introduces the major second, D major.

The most important element of the song, which was subsequently widely sampled, is its twin inter-locking bass lines, played by Herbie Flowers on double bass and overdubbed on fretless bass.

The repeating bass line motif provides an ideal basis for beat matching, as we will see in chapter 3.

Song Structure

00:00–00:19: Eight-bar instrumental intro with basses, acoustic guitars, and drums after the first four bars

00:19–00:29: First verse

00:29–00:52: Pre-chorus, chorus followed by a bar without lyrics

00:52–1:01: Second verse

1:01–1:43: Pre-chorus, chorus followed by eight bars of signature vocal motif "Doo, doo-doo" (first sung by Reed, then by female background singers) and a bar without lyrics

1:43–1:52: Third verse, introduction of string line, bass line changes slightly

1:52–2:15: Pre-chorus, chorus followed by a bar without lyrics

2:15–2:24: Fourth verse, bass line gets more rhythmic

2:24–2:47: Pre-chorus, chorus followed by a bar without lyrics

2:47–2:56: Fifth verse

2:56–3:37: Pre-chorus, chorus followed by twelve bars of signature vocal motif "Doo, doo" and a bar without lyrics

3:37–End: Tenor saxophone solo to fade out

Module 2. Second Song Analysis: A Tribe Called Quest—"Can I Kick It?"

A Tribe Called Quest–"Can I Kick It?"

Stemming from Queens, NY, A Tribe Called Quest is widely considered to be one of the most important hip-hop groups of all time. Their style is marked by a playful and intelligent lyrical approach rapped over low-key and bass-heavy beats.

"Can I Kick It?" is the third single from the group's debut album *People's Instinctive Travels and the Paths of Rhythm*. The song also contains samples by English rocker Ian Dury, keyboardist Dr. Lonnie Smith, and Russian classical composer Sergei Prokofiev, but the characteristic sample from the song is lifted from Lou Reed's "Walk on the Wild Side" bass lines.

Song Structure

0:00–0:19: Eight-bar intro consisting of a two-bar bass sample, looped four times. Acoustic guitar in the background strumming is also part of the sample.

0:19–0:48: Drum loop is added, with vinyl scratching. Main vocal hook "Can I Kick It?—Yes, you can!" arriving at 0:28

0:48–1:27: Drum loop continues on its own with first rap verse. Bass sample reappears at 1:08.

1:27–1:46: Mini interlude with organ and vocal samples, with additional scratching

1:46–2:05: Main bass and acoustic guitar sample reintroduced on its own for eight bars

2:05–2:34: Drum loop added, with more scratching. Main vocal hook "Can I Kick It?—Yes, you can!" arriving at 2:15.

2:34–3:14: Drum loop continues on its own with second rap verse. Bass sample reappears at 2:38, but chopped up at first this time.

3:15–3:32: Mini interlude with organ and vocal samples, with additional scratching

3:32–End: Main bass and acoustic guitar sample reintroduced on its own for eight bars, then drum loop gradually faded in

This song provides plenty of opportunities to beat match in and out of it since it has numerous sections where the bass/acoustic guitar and the drum samples happen on their own.

Module 3. One Way of Mixing the Two Songs Together

Here is one way of mixing these two songs together. It is by no means the only way, but works quite effectively.

First, let's decide on the best tempo possible to go from one song to the next. The tempo of the original studio version of "Walk on the Wild Side" is 104 BPM, and the tempo of the original studio version of "Can I Kick It?" is 97 BPM.

If you are able to easily tweak the tempo of "Wild Side" and have access to a BPM counter, then setting a tempo of 100 BPM seems to be the best compromise for both songs. Remember, it's best to stay close to the original tempo of the songs, in order to preserve sound quality.

Start "Wild Side" then cue "Can I Kick It?" on headphones, press play, and adjust your tempo right away. Practice launching the "Can I Kick It?" intro several times until your tempo is perfectly matched.

When "Wild Side" reaches the 1:00, get ready and try launching "Can I Kick It?" exactly when Lou Reed says "Hey babe, take a walk on the wild side" at 1:05.

Quickly make sure the two bass lines are lined up in your headphones and progressively turn up the volume on "Can I Kick It?" with the low end turned all the way down. Then, progressively turn down the low end on "Wild Side" while bringing it up on "Can I Kick It?"

In a perfect world, the transition happens as the "Can I Kick It?—Yes, you can" lyric arrives when the female background vocalists are singing "Doo doo doo" on "Wild Side." If, for some reason, you didn't manage to line everything up in time, just turn the channel for "Kick It" back down and keep practicing matching things up. You'll get another chance when the next chorus with "Doo doo doos" starts again at 3:00. When the Tribe track is correctly launched and you have turned down the low end on "Wild Side," just turn it off completely and you're done!

Introduction to Set 2

Hip-hop is considered one of the most difficult genres to mix because, unlike mixing house music, mixing hip-hop typically requires some degree of proficiency in turntablism. In addition, hip-hop music is usually slower, hovering between 80 and 100 BPM, whereas house music usually pulsates at around 115 to 130 BPM. Contrary to what most people might think, it is actually more difficult to blend slower tracks than faster ones because more precision is required to successfully set a slower tempo for beat matching.

Transitioning between two hip-hop tracks typically involves well-timed drops, quick fades, tempo changes, and/or scratches, among other skills. Generally, many vocal versions of hip-hop tracks are replete with lyrics and offer a few instrumental breaks that can make transitioning a bit easier. The additional presence of rapped lyrics can create potential issues that a DJ may need to consider.

Too often, an inexperienced DJ (or sometimes a foreign one, who may not realize the importance attached to strong language in the U.S.) might not remember that a good portion of the tracks may contain strong language, rendering said tracks inappropriate for certain functions and venues. Therefore, it is important for a DJ to understand the extent to which profanity is tolerated in each setting. The need to acquire two versions of his/her favorite hip-hop tracks—"explicit" and "clean" versions—can become costly.

Many hip-hop tracks contain a chorus that is sung, so the musical issue of harmonic compatibility could also become problematic. Song A may sound like it could blend well with the instrumental portion of song B; however, the key of the chorus vocals in song B may clash with song A once those vocals begin.

Additionally, a disturbing trend among hip-hop specialists is to equate being a good DJ with "scratching" a lot, a practice often resulting in far too much scratching overall. While scratching can be used creatively to enhance a dance-oriented hip-hop set, it should be used sparingly as most audiences are primarily interested in listening to the song itself and not to the scratching skills of the DJ. As is true for many things in life, the "less is more" approach should apply, unless the style of music you are playing is centered on turntablism.

Finally, without generalizing, crowds expecting hip-hop music have a tendency to be rowdier than others. For this reason, and because of some of the more controversial attitudes promoted by certain hip-hop artists, the DJ has a real responsibility to keep the lyrical content he/she is ultimately responsible for broadcasting under control. Obviously, a DJ should be free to spin whatever he/she feels like, but topics such as glorification of violence, homophobia, and blatant disrespect to the female gender might encourage unfortunate behavior from certain crowds, especially if alcohol consumption is added to the mix.

Module 4. First Song Analysis: Notorious B.I.G.—"Hypnotize"

Notorious B.I.G.—"Hypnotize"

Widely hailed as one of the greatest MCs of all-time, Biggie Smalls, born Christopher Wallace, became a central figure in the East Coast hip-hop scene and increased New York's visibility at a time when West Coast artists were dominating the airwaves.

The song "Hypnotize" was the first single from Biggie Smalls' *Life After Death* album, released in 1996. It reached number one on the Billboard Hot 100 and gave back-to-back No. 1 hits to Sean "Diddy" Combs' Bad Boys record label.

The rhythm track of "Hypnotize" is based on "Rise," an instrumental track by jazz musician Herb Alpert, which was a No. 1 hit in 1979. The chorus of the song is sung by Total, and contains an interpolation of "La Di Da Di" by Doug E. Fresh and Slick Rick.

Song Structure
00:00–00:06: Two-bar instrumental loop
00:06–00:51: First verse
00:51–1:11: Vocal chorus
1:11–1:57: Second verse
1:57–2:18: Vocal chorus
2:18–2:58: Third verse
2:58–End: Vocal chorus

Module 5. Second Song Analysis: Jay-Z—"I Just Wanna Love U"

Jay-Z—"I Just Wanna Love U"

Shawn Carter, better known as Jay-Z, is one of the most successful hip-hop artists of all time, winning twenty-one GRAMMY Awards® and selling fifty million albums worldwide, in addition to becoming a successful entrepreneur.

"I Just Wanna Love U (Give It 2 Me)" was released as the first single from Jay-Z's 2000 album *The Dynasty: Roc La Familia*. Produced by The Neptunes, it features a chorus sung by Neptunes member Pharrell Williams. The single became the first Jay-Z single to reach No. 1 on the Hip-Hop/R&B chart.

The song contains samples from "Give It to Me Baby" by Rick James, "The World Is Filled…" by The Notorious B.I.G., and "I Wish" by Carl Thomas.

Song Structure

0:00–0:10: Four-bar intro
0:10–0:39: Vocal chorus
0:39–1:18: First verse
1:18–1:38: Vocal chorus
1:38–2:18: Second verse
2:18–2:56: Vocal chorus
2:56–3:06: Short third verse
3:06–3:16: The second part of the third verse is rapped by Jay-Z and doubled by Pharrell Williams' singing voice.
3:16–End: Chorus

Module 6. One Method for Mixing the Two Songs Together

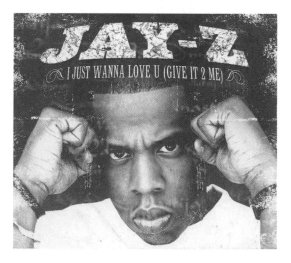

Master Tempo

Beat matching these two songs gives the DJ the perfect opportunity to use the Master Tempo function on the Pioneer CDJ units.

Because the songs are based on the same key, but not the same tempo ("Hypnotize"'s tempo is 94 BPM, while "Wanna Love U"'s is 98 BPM), pressing this button will keep the song in key while letting the DJ alter the tempo of the track.

For this reason, the choice of tempo to beat match the songs is less important. Because Biggie's track's bass line is so powerful when played slowly, let's keep it at its original tempo of 94 BPM.

Start playing "Hypnotize." While it is playing through the speakers, immediately start cueing the first "Wanna Love U" chorus over your headphones, having set the tempo at 94 BPM and having pressed the Master Lock button. Fine-tune the tempo fader on the CDJ so that it exactly matches the tempo of "Hypnotize."

When the tracks are perfectly adjusted, loop "Wanna Love U"'s eight-bar chorus using the CDJ's loop buttons, and store it in the CDJ's memory bank. (Both choruses last exactly eight bars and span over twenty seconds, except for the last chorus of "Hypnotize," which lasts sixteen bars.)

Since it is generally not recommended to have two lyrical verses playing at the same time, it might be fun to play the verses from the first song while switching to the chorus of the second song.

Press the Play button each time the chorus comes around on "Hypnotize" to launch the "Wanna Love U" chorus loop. Since the choruses have exactly the same length (eight bars/twenty seconds), the verses of "Hypnotize" will naturally start again as the choruses for "Wanna Love U" end. Make sure to sample the first "Wanna Love U" chorus, and keep "Wanna Love U" playing once "Hypnotize" is over so the song can keep going on its own.

Module 7. EQ vs. Filters

What are the differences between EQs and filters?

Using EQ

EQs (short for equalizers) act as volume controls on different frequency ranges. Most DJ mixers will feature two, three, or four control knobs to adjust the levels of the different frequencies of each channel.

Assuming the DJ is playing a set of recent, confirmed dance-floor crowd-pleasers that were obtained on digital formats, there might not be the need to use EQing other than for creative reasons. Technically, these songs are likely to have been recorded using similar compression, and therefore having overall similar sound. However, if the DJ is playing an assortment of tracks covering several styles and eras, on a variety of formats (such as vinyl mixed in with CDs), then clever use of EQing will be crucial. Mixing these varied kinds of tracks won't be easy, for they will have been mixed with different stylistic goals in mind, on different gear, at different times.

EQing will serve to harmonize these different tracks and make them sound like they belong together in a set.

Matching and harmonizing EQ ranges on top of overall track levels will help keep consistent energy levels on the dance floor. For example, an incredible but older 1980s house track might not "thump" as hard as today's productions, but a slight increase on the lower frequency EQ knob might compensate for this. If vintage vinyl records sound a little harsh compared to the polished productions of high-quality digital files, adjusting the mediums will likely help.

Using Filters

Filters are similar to EQs because they also alter sound by modifying its frequencies. However, filters cut the volume of all frequencies heard above and/or below a defined point in the frequency range (known as the "cutoff point"), whereas EQs only affect the volume of pre-determined, fixed, frequency ranges (such as low, mids, and highs). Filters do not control the volume of frequencies, only the frequencies at which the cut is made.

Module 8. Using EQs Creatively: Four Techniques

Full Frequency Mixing

When multiple tracks belong to a similar genre, some DJs like to roughly set their EQ settings and then primarily use the volume faders. Although they might make minor EQ adjustments to balance out songs, EQ swapping or full EQ cuts won't generally be used with this technique. "Full frequency" mixing is popular with house music DJs looking to mix their tracks as seamlessly and imperceptibly as possible.

EQ Blending

When trying to mix a track with mid-range signature riffs, such as a guitar loop, with another track with a catchy vocal hook, full frequency mixing might result in overcrowding in the mids range. When playing the two tracks at the same time, it will be necessary to cut down the mids on the first track in order to leave room for the oncoming vocals. However, careful adjustment is necessary because cutting too much mids on the first track might result in a "hollow" effect where too much sonic information is missing between the low and high range.

Low End Swapping

Swapping low ends is a proven technique that is one of most DJs' favorite ways of blending tracks, particularly when dealing with signature bass lines. As with the previous techniques, it will be important to cut enough low end on the first track to "make room" for the upcoming bass line on the new track. Bass frequencies often carry most of the energy of dance music tracks but can sound very muddy when played simultaneously, so careful adjustment is again needed.

Tone Matching

This technique is essential when mixing tracks in different genres and playing on different formats (mixing vinyl with digital tracks, for instance). Using EQ will create a smooth transition between glossy, recent digital tracks and older classics on vinyl. In this situation, cutting the mids out of older songs will allow more gain overall. Increasing higher frequencies on vinyl tracks is usually an effective way to compensate for the limitation presented by the medium as vinyl can only contain a limited amount of higher frequency information.

Location on the Mixer

Although knob configurations vary slightly from mixer to mixer, filter controls usually consist of a single rotary knob and an on/off switch. The knob controls the frequency of the filter cutoff point, not volume. The range covered by filters is usually between about 30 Hz and 20 kHz, which roughly corresponds to the range of frequencies that are audible to the human ear. The cutoff point can be placed anywhere in this range and, therefore, covers the frequencies of all music audible to humans.

The image on the preceding page shows the filter layout on a Pioneer DJM 900 NXS2, with its four rotary knobs below each of the mixer's four channels. Filters can be applied to each channel. When used in conjunction with EQs, filters provide ultimate control over the music's audio frequencies.

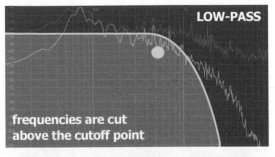

LOW-PASS

frequencies are cut above the cutoff point

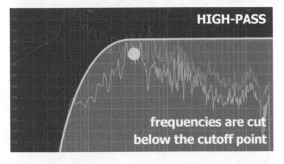

HIGH-PASS

frequencies are cut below the cutoff point

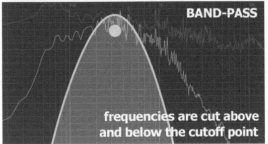

BAND-PASS

frequencies are cut above and below the cutoff point

Low-Pass Filter

A low-pass filter cuts all frequencies heard above the cutoff point. Closing a low-pass filter (by turning down the filter control knob on the mixer) will remove higher frequency sounds like snares and hi-hats. Closing it more will leave the low frequency bass notes and kicks. Closing it all the way will remove all frequencies so the signal will be silent.

High-Pass Filter

The exact opposite of the low-pass filter is a high-pass filter, which cuts off the volume of all frequencies below the cutoff point. Closing a high-pass filter (turning the knob up) will remove low frequencies first and high frequencies last.

This is a commonly used setting. It enables quick and smooth removal of sub-bass frequencies. Drops can be achieved easily by gradually applying a high-pass filter, then completely turning it off to release the subs once again.

Band-Pass Filter

A band-pass filter is a combination of both a high-pass and a low-pass filter. It will remove all frequencies heard both above and below the cutoff point. Adjusting this filter will gradually isolate a certain frequency in the mix. There is no band-pass filter on Pioneer mixers.

Unit Six: Vinyl Emulation Software

Description

In this unit, you will learn about the historical significance of vinyl emulation software and become familiar with the various components that comprise a Serato DJ setup.

Upon completion of this unit, you should be able to:

- Understand the historical chronological order (and cultural significance) of vinyl emulation software

- Name and install the various elements within a basic Serato DJ setup

Module 1. A Brief History of Vinyl Emulation Software

Overview

Thursday March 25th
10pm
$5 / 21+

Last Call

Bleek & Sputnik (Live)
Mathieu Schreyer
KCRW (Guest Dj Set)

Little Temple
4519 Santa Monica Blvd
Los Angeles, CA 90029

Video 19

Ex. 6

Vinyl emulation software allows the user to physically manipulate the playback of digital audio files on a computer using turntables, CD players, or controllers as an interface.

This allows the user to maintain the hands-on control and feel of DJing with vinyl and has the added advantage of using turntables to play back audio recordings not available in physical formats, such as commercial CDs or vinyl. This method allows DJs to scratch, beat match, and perform other tricks and feats reserved to the turntablist, tricks that would be impossible using only a conventional keyboard-and-mouse computer interface or less tactile control devices. This technology is referred to as DVS for either digital vinyl system or digital vinyl software.

Vinyl emulation typically uses special vinyl records (Ex. 6) played on vinyl turntables, such as the SL 1200 by Technics. However, special CD records can also be used with CD players, such as the CDJ-2000 NX2 by Pioneer. Also, an ever-growing number of controllers featuring disc-shaped platters can control vinyl emulation software, removing the need for controlling records entirely.

In the case of vinyl or CD-controlled systems, analog audio signals known as "timecode" are recorded on the discs. The signal emanating from these recordings is then routed to an analog-to-digital converter (usually a USB interface or multi-channel soundcard). This converter then sends the digitized timecode information to the software, which translates the signal into corresponding changes in the playback speed, direction, and position of a digital audio file.

The manipulated audio output of the program is then sent back through the computer's sound card or digital-to-analog converter sind can be routed to an audio mixer where it can be mixed like any other analog audio signal. The result is digital audio playback that sounds like music manipulated by an analog vinyl recording.

FinalScratch

Developed with input from Techno and House music legends Richie Hawtin and John Acquaviva, the first digital vinyl emulation product was named FinalScratch. This product was announced by Dutch company N2IT in 1998 at the COMDEX convention in Las Vegas, NV. Originally developed on the now-defunct BeOS operating system, the software lacked a real user interface and was little more than a glorified mp3 player, a far cry from modern versions of Serato and Traktor (see Ex. 6.1, a photo taken in April, 1999 showing a BeOS-based prototype). FinalScratch was then developed onto the open-source Linux OS.

Ex. 6.1

Ex. 6.2

FinalScratch was bought by Stanton Magnetics who released the first complete commercial FinalScratch product in time for the January, 2002 NAMM show, FinalScratch 1.0.

Thanks to a collaboration with Native Instruments, version 1.5 (Ex. 6.2) introduced a more usable version of the DJ software and released it in 2003. This software, as well as its compatibility with Windows and MacOS, made FinalScratch a mainstream solution for modern DJs.

FinalScratch 2 (Ex. 6.3) featured a high-end Firewire audio device as well as a much improved version of the DVS software. Unfortunately, disagreements between Stanton and Native Instruments eventually led to a lengthy legal battle effectively ending support and development for FinalScratch. Native Instruments subsequently developed its Traktor software on its own, which ultimately became a significant player in the DVS market.

Ex. 6.3

Serato DJ

Video 20

Although developed in 2004, Serato DJ's predecessor, Serato Scratch Live, quickly became a major player in the vinyl emulation software market. Developed by New Zealand-based Serato Audio Research, and distributed by and licensed exclusively to hardware maker Rane, Serato Scratch Live offered essentially the same functionalities as FinalScratch. However, in contrast to the tedious FinalScratch challenge-and-response web-based authorization process, necessitating both software and hardware registrations, Serato made its Scratch Live software available for free, allowing familiarization with the software although the user still needed a compatible USB interface to fully unlock the two-deck vinyl emulation features. Serato tremendously benefited from the confusion surrounding the FinalScratch legal battles between Stanton and Native Instruments, and its Serato DJ program quickly became ubiquitous in DJ circles. In 2013, Serato decided to end support for Serato Scratch Live in 2015 and continues to develop its sister applications, Serato DJ Pro and Serato DJ Lite.

Video 21

Video 22

Module 2. The Serato DJ Setup: Components

In addition to the components already covered in Unit 1: History and Equipment, such as vinyl turntables like the Technics SL 1200, CD turntables such as the Pioneer CDJ-2000 NXS2, DJ mixers such as the Pioneer DJM-900 NXS2, slipmats, and DJ headphones, this chapter will cover the different equipment options available to operate Serato DJ.

Vinyl turntables, CD players, and dedicated controllers can control Serato DJ. However, all these controllers need to connect to the computer via interfaces or mixers.

Rane Interfaces

Serato's hardware partner, Rane, manufactures most of the external interfaces built for Serato DJ. Here is an overview of these interfaces:

Rane SL-2

The SL-2 (Ex. 6.4), replacing the now discontinued SL-1, packs a lot of power for its small size. Boasting high-quality 48 kHz, 24-bit audio, the SL-2 allows for two-deck mixing on turntables or CD decks. In addition, the software allows analog-through connections, which make "real" vinyl or CD playback possible. Its low latency USB 2.0 drivers ensure optimal response, and the unit comes with ASIO and CoreAudio drivers making studio production with third-party software possible. Weighing in at only five pounds, this unit is easy to carry.

Ex. 6.4

Rane SL-3

The SL-3 (Ex. 6.5) is a professional 24-bit DJ interface with studio-grade phono pre-amps for superior sound. Extra aux inputs and outputs allow for an optional third deck, recording, or output for external units. The SL-3's inputs can welcome any input combination, CD or vinyl. Its high output improves the ability to easily match levels of various source types. Its auxiliary inputs can be used for session recording or LiveFeed, and its auxiliary outputs can be assigned to the Serato DJ's Sample player.

Ex. 6.5

Rane SL-4

The SL-4 (Ex. 6.6) offers superior sound with 96 kHz sample rate, 24-bit audio processing, and galvanic isolation to eliminate computer noise and interference. Providing inputs for four turntables or CD decks switchable in any combination, this unit also allows for seamless DJ changeover and back-to-back performance thanks to its two USB ports. It also acts as a 10-in and 10-out USB sound card compatible with any software supporting ASIO or CoreAudio drivers.

Ex. 6.6

Rane Mixers for Serato DJ

Rane also builds a range of high-end mixers with Serato DJ connectivity built in, including:

Rane Seventy-Two

The Rane Seventy-Two (Ex. 6.7) features two USB ports and a 4.3-inch color touchscreen showing moving waveforms and cue points. This Serato DJ Pro compatible mixer has 16 Akai Pro MPC performance pads with RGB backlight, two internal FLEX FX engines, and stacked Serato FX. It also has a footswitch for more FX and MIDI Control options, Serato DJ Pro Sampler level and filter control knobs, two microphone inputs with Duck and Custom Echo, and three-Band Isolator EQs and High-Pass/Low-Pass for each channel. Last but not least, it sports high-end Mag Three contactless tension-adjustable faders.

Ex. 6.7

Rane Sixty-Two

This Rane Sixty-Two (Ex. 6.8) supports two computers, two-deck vinyl simulation, and Sample Player control as well as direct control of over forty DJ software controls. Its internal effects include Filter, Flanger, Phaser, Echo, Robot, and Reverb. Like the Seventy-Two, it offers support for ASIO and CoreAudio drivers, external analog inserts for analog effects, processors, and a USB insert for software effects.

Controllers

Using the new Serato DJ software, controller DJs can now enjoy the power of Serato with light and easy-to-carry controllers. Controller devices typically feature rotary platters as well as a central master fader mixer section. They often offer cue as well as effect buttons. Here are a few controllers compatible with Serato DJ:

Ex. 6.8

Numark Mixtrack Pro 3

The Mixtrack Pro 3 (Ex. 6.9) features two channels, 5-inch metal jog wheels, dedicated filter knobs for each channel, a multi-function touch strip for dynamic FX control and track search, sixteen performance pads, 1/4-inch and 1/8-inch headphone connections, and a mic input, and it includes the entry-level Serato DJ Lite. It is also upgrade-ready for Serato DJ Pro. A remix toolkit called "Prime Loops" is also included. The unit offers

Ex. 6.9

RCA, unbalanced outputs, and an integrated 24-bit, 44.1 kHz class-compliant audio interface and can also be used as a MIDI controller.

Video 23

Video 24

Pioneer DDJ-SB2

The DDJ-SB2 (Ex. 6.10) has been upgraded with 4-deck control and dedicated buttons to easily switch between channels. Its key features include tactile performance pads, large jog wheels, trim knobs for dynamic volume control, manual filters on every channel, and a filter fade function to simultaneously control both the volume and bass filters. The unit comes stocked with Serato DJ Lite and a 24-bit/44.1 kHz sound card.

Ex. 6.10

Numark NS-7 III

The NS-7 III (Ex. 6.11) is Numark's flagship DJ controller. It features four channels, 7-inch motorized turntables with real vinyl and slipmats, touch-sensitive knobs and filters, velocity-sensitive performance pads, and three display screens. It offers the ability to connect vinyl turntables and CD players, as well as other media players. Its mixer can operate with or without a computer, in standalone mode. It also comes with Serato DJ Pro, a Pitch 'n Time expansion pack, and an FX suite powered by iZotope. In addition, this unit features many advanced

Ex. 6.11

items, including extensive MIDI mapping, up to eight cue points, four-deck control, recording, beatgrid detection, and editing.

Pioneer DDJ-SZ

The Pioneer DDJ-SZ (Ex. 6.12) features full-size, aluminum jog wheels inherited from the CDJ-2000 NXS, illuminated and highly accurate digital track position indicators, large performance pads, and two USB sound cards for smooth DJ-changeover. It also offers support for DVS control, which allows DJs to connect CD players or vinyl turntables that can be used to operate Serato DJ Pro, or it can be used as a stand-alone mixer. It also features MIDI mapping, the Pitch 'n Time expansion

Ex. 6.12

pack, four-deck control, up to eight nameable cue points, beatgrid detection and editing, recording, and high quality hardware and build. It sports XLR and RCA master outs, 1/4-inch booth outs, one 1/4-inch and one XLR mic input, and phono and line RCA inputs.

Module 3. Installation

Start by making sure that all the elements are laid on a sturdy, flat, and stable surface and that no cables are tangled under the feet of the turntables, controllers, or under the mixer.

With a vinyl/Serato setup or a CDJ/Serato setup, plug the RCA cables from the turntables into the "1" and "2" or "Deck 1" and "Deck 2" inputs of the USB interface, matching colors accordingly. The nature of the input ("Line" or "Phono") can be selected on the interface.

If using vinyl turntables, connect the ground wire from the turntables to the mixer. The appropriate connecting spot will usually be a twistable knob that the flat metal U-shaped cable tip can slide under. Once the tip is in place, tighten the knob, securing the cable firmly into place. Grounding is important to prevent feedback, distortion, or other interferences.

If using a controller, just connect it to the USB port of your computer. This will make the unit recognizable by Serato DJ and will also provide power to the controller. Optional power supplies are sometimes provided as a more reliable power source than USB.

Once all the elements are installed and powered off, make sure that all gains and volume controls are set to zero on the mixer. This prevents potentially damaging voltage surges from reaching the mixer's inputs.

With a vinyl setup, it's important to balance needles for proper operation. This step will ensure that there is adequate pressure on the record to prevent skipping, but not so much as to cause excessive wear on the needle or on the record itself. Adjust the cylinder weight (Ex. 6.13) on the back of the tone arm until the arm floats in the center, not tipping to either side, then roll on about three grams of pressure using the gauge on the weight.

Turn the turntables' and the mixer's power on, put a record on, and press play. Gradually increase the level on the mixer's channel until the meters are just below the red. Do the same for the other turntable.

Once the gain levels are set, increase the master volume to an adequate level. Don't turn the master volume all the way or the music might distort. Set it to about 50% and adjust the volume on the PA system or the headphones level. This will leave headroom on the mixer's volume, which will allow for easy adjustment during your set if needed.

Set the EQs to zero to prevent excessive coloration of the sound. Starting from neutral settings will allow you to hear the music as it has been recorded. You can then make adjustments as you see fit to harmonize the sound between various recordings, thus easing the transitions between them.

Ex. 6.13

Unit Seven: Working with Vinyl Emulation Software

Description

In this unit, you will learn about calibrating your vinyl or CD players for optimum use with Serato DJ. You will also learn about importing, preparing, and analyzing music files. Playback control and control records and CDs will be discussed.

Upon completion of this unit, you should be able to:

- Calibrate vinyl and CD players with Serato DJ
- Import, prepare, and analyze music files
- Comprehend Playback control within Serato DJ
- Mix with one CD player or vinyl turntable

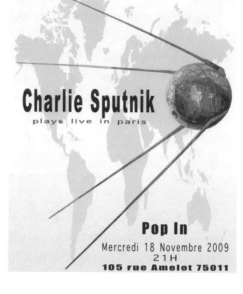

Module 1. Calibration of Your Vinyl or CDJ Setup

When using vinyl turntables or CDJs in conjunction with Serato DJ, it is necessary to correctly process the audio signal coming from the control vinyl or CDs because Serato DJ needs to calibrate this signal to function properly. The control signal is made up of two elements, the directional tone, which indicates the speed and direction of the record, and the noise map, which indicates the exact position of the needle on the vinyl. The noise generated by the record needs to be sufficiently loud to be processed by the software, so it is important to make sure the signal is properly calibrated.

Ex. 7

Once the CD players or vinyl turntables are properly connected, place the needle on the vinyl record while the turntable is stopped. Similarly, press the pause button on the CD player. Click and hold the "Estimate" slider under the scopes (Ex. 7).

Start either turntables or CD players. Two green, circle-like shapes will appear on the scope. These shapes should be round, and the lines should be as clean as possible. Use the L/R and the P/A balance controls on the sides of the scopes to make the lines as round as possible. The percentage numbers in the lower right corners will indicate the quality of the tracking. Those should be between 85% and 100%.

Once the calibration has been made, stop the records. The number on the top-right corner of the scope view, indicating the RPM should be at 0.0. In the event that number isn't 0.0, move the "Estimate" slider until it stays at 0.0.

Module 2. Importing, Preparing, and Analyzing Tracks

Importing and Loading

Video 25

Ensure the USB cable connecting your Serato DJ device is disconnected from the computer. Click on the "Files" button (Ex. 7.1) located below the central wave display. Navigate and locate the folder containing the music files you would like to import. Drag

Ex. 7.1

this folder onto the "All…" icon, which is located at the very top of the crates and playlists window on the left side of the screen. All the tracks on your library should be visible when you press the "All…" icon. Connect the USB linking your Serato DJ device to your computer and ensure that two circular Virtual Decks appear on the right and the left of your screen. Tracks can be loaded by individually highlighting them, then dragging them from the track list area onto either Virtual Deck. Highlighted tracks can also be loaded automatically on either deck by pressing SHIFT + left arrow or SHIFT + right arrow. The track will start playing once the controller, turntable, or CD player is started.

Preparing and Analyzing Tracks

File analysis is necessary before playing your music through Serato DJ. This process will determine the tracks' tempi (BPM), key signature, and whether or not any files are corrupted and cannot be played. It will also save song waveform overviews and auto-gain information.

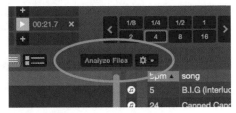

Ex. 7.2

To analyze files, disconnect any hardware from your computer once more. Click the "Analyze Files" (Ex. 7.2) button to the left of the main screen. This will create waveform overviews for all the files in your library. Crates, files, or folders can also be dragged and dropped onto this button at any time.

Upon analysis, it is possible that corrupt files are found. If found, these files must be deleted immediately because they can cause Serato DJ to crash, regardless of whether they are played or not. A "lightning" icon appearing to the left of the file name will mark corrupt files.

Serato DJ will automatically calculate the tempo values (BPM) for files as long as the "Set Auto BPM" box to the right of the "Analyze Files" button is checked. This information will be saved as long as prior BPM information isn't already present.

Module 3. Playback Control: Control Records and CDs

Serato Control Record

When controlling Serato DJ via vinyl turntables, one must use Serato DJ Control Vinyl. A Serato Control Vinyl (Ex. 7.3) has two sides, side A lasting ten minutes and side B lasting fifteen minutes. The vinyl can function at either 33 or 45 BPM. When the record reaches its end, Serato DJ will automatically switch to Internal (INT) mode to prevent the song from stopping. Side A contains a vinyl scroll section at its end, which allows selecting and loading tracks without having to touch the computer.

Ex. 7.3

Serato Control CD

The Serato Control CD (Ex. 7.4) has two tracks, one lasting fifteen minutes and the second one containing vinyl scroll. The vinyl scroll can be employed via stopping the deck, selecting track 2 on the CD, and spinning the CDJ platter forward or backward. This will go up or down on the list of tracks in your library. Once the track you would like to load is highlighted, select track 1 and the track will be loaded. This works in a similar way on a vinyl deck, just place the needle on the section at the very end of the record, move the vinyl to scroll through tracks, and put the needle back at the beginning of the record.

Ex. 7.4

Module 4. Mixing with One CD Player or Vinyl Turntable

When using vinyl turntables or CDJs to control Serato DJ, it is still possible to mix, beat match, and scratch if one of the turntables breaks down or if the user only has one CD player handy.

First, check the "Lock Playing Deck" and the "Instant Doubles" options under the DJ Preferences tab (Ex. 7.5) in the Setup screen.

Make sure your CD player or turntable is connected to the Right deck.

Then, load a track onto the Right deck, start playing it, and set the Left deck to Internal ("INT") mode. Load the same track on the Left deck: it will "mirror" the Right deck and play at exactly the same location and pitch as the track on the Right deck.

You can now rapidly switch the faders on your mixer and have the Left deck play out loud; this shouldn't affect the audio in any way since the tracks should be perfectly in sync at this stage.

Load a new track on the Right deck and repeat the process.

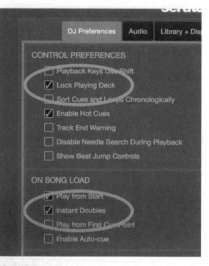

Ex. 7.5

8 Unit Eight: Vinyl Emulation Software: The Main Screen of Serato DJ Pro

Description

In this unit, you will learn about each of the controls within the Main Screen of Serato DJ Pro.

Upon completion of this unit, you should be able to:

Understand (and be able to use) the functions contained within Serato DJ Pro's Main Screen.

Module 1. The Virtual Deck and Waveform Displays

The Virtual Deck

Serato DJ Pro usually features two (sometimes four) Virtual Decks (Ex. 8), which are a graphic representation of the two (or four) physical decks comprising a digital DJing setup.

The center dial of each deck shows time elapsed, time remaining, and BPM information including pitch adjustment, range, and the percentage of pitch variation compared to the original BPM of the track.

Ex. 8

Tempo Matching Display

When in "Horizontal Mode," this display (Ex. 8.1) sits above the audio waveforms window. The software will detect beats in each track and will place a row of red peaks (for the left player) above a row of yellow peaks (for the right one). The peaks will line up when the tracks are beat matched, so this visual aide is helpful to the user.

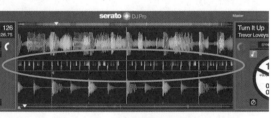

Ex. 8.1

Track Overview Displays

Directly above and below the Tempo Matching display, waveforms showing an overview of the entire tracks selected help the user finding different sections of the tracks. Transitions can therefore be anticipated and planned ahead of time thanks to the Track Overview displays (Ex. 8.2). The waveforms are colored based on the spectrum range of the music played: low frequencies and bass sounds will be colored red, mediums will be shaded green, and trebles will be blue.

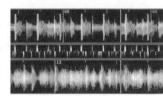

Ex. 8.2

The Main Waveform and Beat Matching Displays

In the middle of the main screen sits the Main Waveform display. The top waveform represents the track being played on the left deck, and the bottom waveform represents the track being played on the right deck. The same colors are used as in the Track Overview displays to show the frequency range of individual sounds. Clicking on the waveforms will allow audio "scrubbing" and is helpful to set cue points. Zooming is possible by using the + and − keys.

The Beat Matching display is sandwiched between the two main waveforms and shows the position of beats within the track. This display is helpful when beat matching as the beats displayed will be lined up when the two tracks selected are beat matched.

Using the Displays When Beat Matching

First, make sure the peaks shown on the Tempo Matching display are lined up. This will verify that the BPM of each track is the same. Second, make sure the beats shown on the Beat Matching display are staying aligned over time and not veering away from each other. This will ensure that the tracks are solidly beat matched. Fine-tuning may be required for tracks to stay beat matched for extended periods of time.

Module 2: Main Screen Indicators and Buttons

Output Levels

Ex. 8.3   Serato DJ Pro has individual output level dials to adjust the gain of each track as well as a Master Output Level (Ex. 8.3) dial that sets the Master volume output of the software to the mixer. In order to avoid distortion, it is best to leave this control at the "Noon" setting.

Key Detection

Ex. 8.4   Serato DJ Pro will automatically determine the track's key as well as its BPM upon import and analysis. The track's key can be found between the track's name and its BPM information (Ex. 8.4).

Tap Tempo

Ex. 8.5   The Tap Tempo (Ex. 8.5) button appears when the BPM of a track has not already been embedded in its metadata. The user can manually input the track's tempo by tapping the track pad or clicking the mouse in time with the track. Serato DJ will then calculate the track's approximate BPM and display it.

Key Lock

Ex. 8.6   Key Lock (Ex. 8.6) is an extremely useful feature that locks the key the track is originally recorded in, regardless of tempo changes by the user. The track's tempo can be increased or decreased without changing its pitch. Shortcuts for the Key Lock feature are F5 for the left deck and F10 for the right deck.

Censor

Ex. 8.7   The Censor function (Ex. 8.7) is only available in Internal ("INT") and Relative ("REL") modes. It is used to mask a section of a song. When this button is pressed and held down, the track plays in reverse, creating a special sound effect. When the user lets go of the button, the track resumes playing at the location the track would have reached if it had kept playing. This function is useful to garble inappropriate language or to avoid playing certain parts of songs.

Eject

Ex. 8.8   Pressing this button (Ex. 8.8) will eject the track currently loaded on either deck.

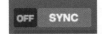 **Autoplay**

Ex. 8.9   When enabled, the Autoplay function (Ex. 8.9), located at the very bottom left of the screen, will automatically load the next song on the list after the current track is finished playing. The Autoplay function is only available in Internal ("INT") and Relative ("REL") modes.

Sync

Ex. 8.10   Pressing the Sync button (Ex. 8.10), located above each virtual deck, will automatically match the BPM values of both tracks, thus rendering beat matching even easier.

Cue Points Panel

Serato DJ Pro allows for the creation of markers within a track called Cue Points (Ex. 8.11). They are very useful as they enable the user to immediately jump to a particular section of a track. These Cue Points can be named and are saved into the track's metadata and can therefore be retrieved the next time the track is loaded.

Ex. 8.11

Loop Panel

Loops of various lengths and type (Ex. 8.12) can be created on the fly using Serato DJ Pro in order to lengthen or emphasize a particular section of a track. These loops are saved into a track's metadata for easy retrieval.

Ex. 8.12

Unit Nine: Display Modes and Playback Modes

Description

In this unit, you will learn the different display options offered by Serato DJ Pro, as well as the various playback modes included within the platform.

Upon completion of this unit, you should be able to:

Use Serato DJ Pro's playback modes: Absolute mode, Relative mode, and Internal mode. We will examine Serato DJ's Thru mode as well.

Module 1. Serato DJ Pro's Display Modes and Library Views

Display Modes

Serato DJ Pro offers five display modes to suit every user's visual preferences.

Library Mode:

This mode puts the emphasis on the library and not on the virtual deck, so information usually present inside the circular decks, such as time remaining, time elapsed, etc. is missing.

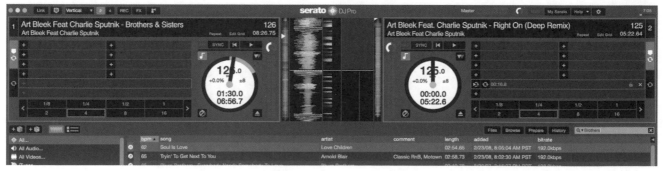

Ex. 9

Vertical Mode:

This mode displays the waveforms vertically, leaving the two virtual decks on each side. The emphasis is placed on the virtual decks and on the information contained inside of the circles.

Ex. 9.1

Horizontal Mode:

This mode displays the waveforms horizontally, leaving the virtual decks on each side.

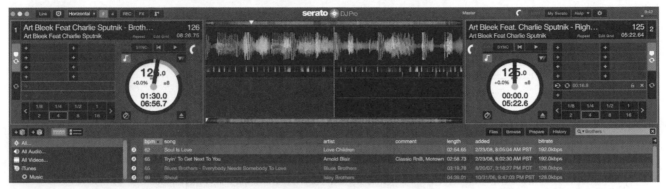

Ex. 9.2

Stack Mode:

This mode stacks the waveforms on top of each other horizontally. The virtual decks are missing some information and are located to the left of the waveforms.

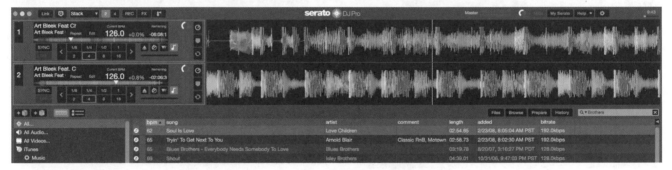

Ex. 9.3

Extended Mode:

This mode displays horizontal waveforms spread across the entire screen.

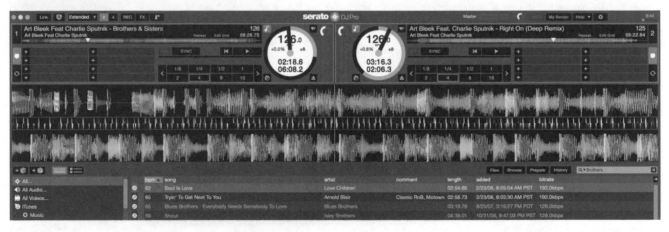

Ex. 9.4

Serato DJ Pro provides the possibility of toggling between any mode and the default Library mode by simply pressing the space bar.

Library Views

Serato DJ Pro offers two different Library views to display track information and art. The different Library views can be selected by pressing the Library view buttons located below the left virtual deck.

 Simple List

The Simple List display shows track information only.

 Album Art List

The Album Art List display shows album art as well as the track information.

Album Art can also be added to any file by clicking and dragging a .jpg or .png file onto a track, provided this track is displayed in one of the Album Art views.

Module 2. Absolute Mode

When used with control records, Serato DJ Pro can be operated using one of three Serato DJ Pro modes. In addition, the software also allows playing regular vinyl or CD recordings via Thru mode.

Ex. 9.5

Absolute Mode ("ABS") is Serato DJ Pro's default mode, and is the mode offering the closest experience to using real vinyl records or real CDs. The entire track is mapped to the record, and lifting the needle while the track is playing will cause the record to stop. Also, picking up the needle and dropping it elsewhere on the record will cause the track playing to jump to that mapped location, exactly as if the user were dropping the needle on a real vinyl.

Absolute Mode is the mode of choice for turntablists, as it reproduces the movement captured by the needle, as if using a vinyl record. Thus, the user will be able to scratch exactly as if he/she were scratching with real vinyl. When the control record reaches its end, Serato DJ Pro automatically switches to Internal mode ("INT") to prevent the track from abruptly stopping. To go back to Absolute Mode, simply lift the tone arm and place the needle back at the beginning of the record.

Press F1 to switch the Left deck into Absolute Mode, or F6 for the Right deck, or press the "ABS" button located towards the top of each Virtual Deck.

Module 3. Relative Mode

Like Absolute Mode, Relative Mode ("REL") also reproduces the movement of the needle on the record and allows for scratching, but unlike Absolute Mode, it doesn't take the placement of the needle on the record into consideration. The user will not be able to pick up the needle and move it to a different part of the song: the record will stop when the needle arm is lifted, but will restart exactly where it stopped when placed back down anywhere on the record. This mode makes scratching easier, as the record will not skip.

Ex. 9.6

Users can switch to Relative Mode by pressing F2 for the Left deck and F7 for the Right deck.

Module 4. Internal Mode

Ex. 9.7

Internal Mode ("INT") allows operating Serato DJ Pro without the help of external controllers or physical decks, such as vinyl turntables or CD players.

Internal Mode features Pitch Slider controls on the side of each Virtual Deck. Clicking and dragging them can manually nudge these sliders upwards and downwards. For more progressive (slower) pitch adjustment, hold the "SHIFT" button while clicking and dragging. Above the Pitch Slider controls, "RANGE" buttons will toggle between ±8%, ±10%, ±16%, and ±50%.

Like Relative Mode ("REL"), Internal Mode adds a few functions:

The "+" and "-" buttons respectively temporarily increase and decrease the speed of the track. This function, known as "Bend Up" or "Bend Down," is equivalent to nudging a vinyl record forward and backwards for adjustment purposes when trying to beat match two tracks. It should only be used when two tracks are playing at the same tempo, but one track is slightly ahead or behind the other track.

To switch to Internal Mode, press F3 for the Left deck and F8 for the Right deck.

Ex. 9.8

Module 5. Thru Mode

A Thru Mode (THRU) option is also present in the Playback Mode drop-down menu on the side of each Virtual Deck. Selecting this option allows playing regular vinyl records or CDs. Clicking on the THRU button causes the main waveform displays to become grayed out. Audio signal will then be sent directly from the user's vinyl or CD players to the DJ mixer and thru the Serato Box's inputs and outputs.

It is important to note when using the THRU function that it is usually safer for a Serato Box to be powered up by using the box's optional external power supply.

To return to one of the three software-controlled Serato DJ Pro modes, just select another Playback Mode.

Unit Ten: Cue Points

10

Description

In this unit, you will learn about the various Cue Point options offered by Serato DJ Pro.

Upon completion of this unit, you should be able to:

Create, trigger, edit, and customize Cue Points within Serato DJ Pro.

Module 1. Creating and Triggering Cue Points

Ex. 10

Video 26

Cue Points are locations set on a track by the user. They are stored with the track information and will appear on the Cue Point column next to each Virtual Deck each time the track is loaded.

Up to eight Cue Points can be set per track by pressing on the "+" sign to the right of the Cue Points column (Ex. 10). A Cue Point will be created at the current playback position on the track.

During playback, pressing the numbers 1 to 5 will create Cue Points 1–5 on the Left deck, and pressing the numbers 6 to 0 will create Cue Points 1–5 on the Right deck. Once a Cue Point has been assigned to a particular slot, it is possible to trigger it by pressing the corresponding number on the keyboard or by pressing the corresponding "HOT CUE" button when using a controller.

It is also possible to create "Hot Cues" on the fly using a controller as the track is playing: Simply press the "HOT CUE" button on your controller on the Virtual Deck of your choice. The "HOT CUE" button will light up to indicate that a Cue Point has been created. These can only be created if the corresponding Cue Point slot is empty.

If a track is paused, pressing and holding a Cue Point play button (or "HOT CUE" button if using a controller) will play the track from the corresponding location. The track will stop playing and revert to the location once the play button (or "HOT CUE" button) is released.

In Internal Mode ("INT"), it is possible to "grab" the audio waveform and "scrub" to find the exact location desired for creating a Cue Point. The user can also zoom in and out of the main audio waveform for greater visual accuracy pressing the SHIFT + "-" or SHIFT + "+" keys.

Cue Points can only be triggered in Relative and Internal mode.

Module 2. Triggering, Editing, and Customizing Cue Points

Ex. 10.1

Video 27

Cue Points colors can be customized by right-clicking on the Cue Point play buttons. When a specific Cue Point is triggered, the stripe at the center of the Virtual Deck will jump to the "noon" position and switch to the color of the corresponding Cue Point (Ex. 10.1).

As the track approaches a specific Cue Point during playback, the stripe's color will grow by a fifth at each rotation until the Cue Point is reached. The colored stripe will then shorten by a fifth at each rotation.

Cue Points can easily be removed and deleted by pressing the "X" to the right of each Cue Point in the Cue Point column. They can also be overwritten with new ones by pressing CTRL + "1" to CTRL + "0."

To label Cue Points and give them a specific name, such as "Top," "Break," "Drop," or "Chorus," just double-click on each Cue Point's time field. Cue Points can also be dragged and dropped in the order the user chooses, and they can also be organized chronologically by clicking on the "Sort Cues Chronologically" in the Playback tab on the Setup screen.

Temporary Cues can be set, but will not be saved with the track information and will not appear when the track is reloaded: Pressing "I" for the Left deck and "K" for the Right deck will create a Temporary Cue, recognizable by a white marker created on the waveform and a white stripe on the Virtual Deck. They will function in a similar manner as regular Cue Points.

Unit Eleven: Loops

11

Description

In this unit, you will learn about the various Looping options offered by Serato DJ Pro.

Upon completion of this unit, you should be able to:

- Create loops, Auto-Loops, and Loop Rolls
- Assign Loop Rolls to MIDI controllers

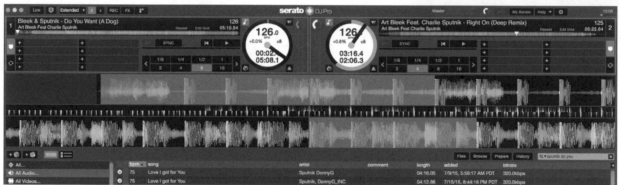

Module 1. Creating Manual Loops

Using loops is useful to extend certain sections of a track or to create new mashups "on the fly." Up to eight loops can be created on each track and saved along with the track information. These loops will appear each time the track is re-loaded. The Looping function is only effective in Relative and Internal Modes when using control records.

When viewing the Cue Panel, the first saved two loops will be visible, for easy access (Ex. 11).

To create a Manual loop, open the Loop Panel next to the Virtual Deck area. Press the "IN" button in the loop panels (Ex. 11.1), which are located on each side of the Virtual Decks. This will create the in-point of the Manual loop. The out-point is selected by pressing the "OUT" button. Pressing the "Loop" button turns loops on or off. If using a controller, the corresponding "IN" and "OUT" buttons can also be used.

Manual loop in-points can be adjusted in the following manner: While the loop is playing, press the "IN" button, which will start blinking. This will stop

Ex. 11

Ex. 11.1

the loop from visually scrolling (although the audio will still play) and will bring the focus on the in-point of the loop, which can be adjusted by pressing the left or the right arrow keys. The left arrow will nudge the in-point earlier, while the right arrow will push it later. Holding the "SHIFT" key while pressing the arrows makes adjustments in larger increments. The same method can be applied for the out-point. To resume scrolling, just press the "IN" button again (or the "OUT" button if you are adjusting the out-point).

The keyboard shortcut to adjust in-points are "O" for the Left deck and "L" for the Right deck.

The keyboard shortcut to adjust out-points are "P" for the Left deck and ";" for the Right deck.

A control vinyl record, control CD, or controller platter can also be used to manually adjust loop in- and out-points: Just click the "IN" button, nudge the record or CD backward or forward towards the desired in-point, and click the "IN" button again to save. The same method can be used to manually adjust the out-point.

The Slot Reloop button will start the loop from the in-point and the Loop on/off button will activate and deactivate the selected loop (Ex. 11.2).

Ex. 11.2

It is possible to double or cut by half the length of a loop on the fly by pressing the 1/2X or the 2X buttons located immediately above the pre-adjusted auto-loop set length values and below the loop list. Corresponding buttons can also be found on most controllers (Ex. 11.3).

Ex. 11.3

Module 2. Auto Loops

Auto-looping is the ability to create up to five loops per Virtual Deck automatically and instantly. This feature is only available to tracks with BPM information.

Serato DJ Pro will automatically determine exact in- and out-points once the user sets the number of beats that should be looped. Loop lengths can be as short as 1/32 of a beat and as long as 32 beats and can be adjusted by pressing the left and the right arrows on either side of the number of beats selected (Ex. 11.3).

Auto-loop in-points are created by clicking on a pre-defined length value and are set to the nearest beat. The out-point of an Auto-loop will be automatically set at the end of the loop, and reflecting the desired loop length. On most controllers, loop-length values are generally assigned to touch sensitive pads and organized in similar patterns as displayed on the screen.

It is possible to create an auto-loop by using the ALT + "1" to ALT + "5" keyboard shortcuts for the Left deck and the ALT + "6" to ALT + "0" shortcuts for the Right deck. Loop length will then correspond to the number of beats displayed on the screen at the time the shortcut is used. For the screen above for example, ALT + "1" would create an 1/8-beat loop and ALT + "5" would create a 2-beat loop.

To turn an active loop off, simply press the selected length value button or pad again.

Module 3. Loop Rolls

Video 28

A Loop Roll is similar to an Auto-loop, but when the loop is turned off, the playback position is resumed to the position the track would have reached if the loop hadn't been enabled. It is similar to the "Censor" function covered in Unit 8, but for loops.

Loop Roll can be selected "on the fly," using the following keyboard shortcuts: CTRL + ALT + 1 to CTRL + ALT + 5 (Left deck) and CTRL + ALT + 6 to CTRL + ALT + 0 (Right deck). Just like Auto-loops, Loop lengths will correspond to the number of beats displayed on the screen at the time the shortcut is used.

The main differences between Auto loops and Loop Rolls is that Loop Rolls will only be enabled while keyboard shortcut combinations are held down. The other main difference, as stated previously, is the momentary nature of the Loop Roll: when the Loop Roll keyboard shortcut combination is released, the track will resume playing at the location it would have reached if it had continued playing uninterrupted. For this reason, Loop Rolls are useful for creating "on-the-fly" rhythmic transitions. For example, a stutter effect can be achieved by selecting a short loop length.

Unit Twelve: Sample Player

Description

In this unit, you will learn about using Serato DJ Pro's internal Sampler Player.

Upon completion of this unit, you should be able to:

- Load and play samples using the Sampler

- Employ the Sampler various controls

- Enhance your set by incorporating samples provided by the Sampler

Module 1. Loading and Playing Samples with the Sampler

Ex. 12

The Sampler (Ex. 12) is an internal sampler allowing the user to load and play eight sources of audio in addition to the two tracks on the main Virtual Decks. Any audio file can be loaded in one of the Sampler eight slots regardless of length. The Sampler main control panel appears when the "Sampler" button is pushed. This button is located above the left virtual deck, to the right of the "FX" button.

Tracks can easily be loaded into the Sampler by selecting a track in the Library and dragging it in one of the Sampler's eight slots. Pressing the Eject button to the right of each slot ejects tracks. Eight tracks can be loaded simultaneously in the eight slots by selecting and dragging them onto the first slot. The keyboard shortcut for loading tracks in the Sampler is CTRL + ALT + "Z" to CTRL + ALT + ",".

Pressing the PLAY button on each slot can play each sample, or you can press the corresponding button on your controller. Pressing the letters "Z" to "," on your computer keyboard to select the slots 1 to 8 can also respectively trigger each sample.

Once the "Instant Double" option is selected in the Setup window, it is possible to instantly double any track playing on the Virtual Decks by dragging and dropping the track onto one of the Sampler's slots. The position, gain, speed, and sync information of the track will be kept when dragging the track. It is also possible to drag a track from a slot to the Virtual Decks or to another slot. This way, a Virtual Deck can be freed up by dragging a track down to an empty Sampler slot after it has been "instant doubled."

Module 2. View Modes and Play Modes

At the bottom right corner of each sample slot, there is a settings wheel button that can alternatively select the Simple or Advanced view modes (Ex. 12.1). The Advanced view mode displays more features than the Simple view mode.

Ex. 12.1

The Sampler has three playback modes:

Trigger Mode

Plays audio until the end of the track. Pressing play again while the track is playing starts playing the track again from the beginning. To stop the track, press either ALT + "PLAY" or ALT + Z for slot 1 to ALT + "," for slot 8.

Hold Mode

Plays the sample as long as the play button is pressed and held. This is equivalent to the "note off" setting found on most hardware samplers.

On/Off Mode

Plays the sample until the end of the track. To stop the sample, press "PLAY" again.

Repeat Button

Right below the playback button, there is a Repeat button (Ex. 12.2). When activated, pressing this button causes the file to repeat when it reaches the end. It is recommended to edit a sample in the Virtual Deck prior to loading into the Sampler to make sure the sample will loop smoothly.

Ex. 12.2

Located to the right of the repeat button, an individual volume knob controls the volume of each loaded sample.

Module 3. Sampler's Advanced Controls

Pitch Controls

In Advanced view mode, the Sampler Pitch Controls include a Pitch Slider, BPM display, "-"/"+" bend/nudge buttons, and key lock control (Ex. 12.3). Clicking and dragging the pitch slider will adjust pitch. For finer adjustments, press "SHIFT" while dragging. Click "-" or "+" to make temporary pitch adjustments (to refine track line-up once both tracks are at the same tempo, for example). Press CTRL while clicking on the slider to reset the pitch to zero. Press the key lock button to lock the track's key regardless of the tempo.

Ex. 12.3

"Play From" Control

The "Play From" control determines the starting point of the sample (Ex. 12.4). The starting point of the file can be the start of the track or any Cue Point or loop in-point. When the starting point is a Cue Point, the sample will play until the end of the track; however, when the starting point is a Loop in-point, the track will play only until the loop's out-point unless the "REPEAT" function is enabled, in which case, the loop will repeat from its in-point. The Cue and Loop information, saved with the track information, will determine the "Play From" option within the Sampler.

Ex. 12.4

Individual Sample Gain and Mute Button

Individual volume knobs are available in each Sampler slot (Ex. 12.5). These are useful to adjust the volume of a sample that is too quiet or too loud. The adjusted value will be saved with the sample file for the next time the sample is loaded. A Mute button is available for each Sampler slot. Control clicking the Mute button will mute the sample for as long as the click is held.

Ex. 12.5

Main Volume, Mute, and Output Selector

Located immediately above the last Sampler slot, Volume, Mute, and Output  controls affect the overall Sampler volume output (Ex. 12.6). Control clicking the **Ex. 12.6** Mute button will mute the Sampler for as long as the click is held. The number of outputs the Sampler can be routed to depends on the user's hardware.

An SL-3 Serato box is used in the example above so the user has the choice of routing the Sampler's output audio to channels 1, 2, or 3. Selecting "M" routes the Sampler's output audio to the Master output of the Serato DJ Pro hardware.

Sample Banks

The Sampler stores its individual samples in four sample banks, labeled A, B, C, and D. These are located at the very left of the Sampler, above the first slot. Each individual sample will be saved along with its settings. Sample bank A loads by default. Each bank can hold up to eight samples, for a total of thirty-two samples available across the four banks. To switch Sample banks, simply choose another letter, representing one of the four banks.

Unit Thirteen: 13 DJ-FX Plug-In

Description

In this unit, you will learn about using Serato DJ Pro's fully customizable internal DJ-FX plug-in.

Upon completion of this unit, you should be able to:

- Use the DJ-FX plug-in in Single FX Mode
- Use the DJ-FX plug-in in Multi FX Mode
- Assign effects and adjust parameters on each deck

Module 1. Single FX Mode

Serato DJ Pro offers two effects units. These effects can only be used when Serato DJ Pro is connected to hardware. The effects panel will appear when the "FX" button, located at the very top of the display towards the left side, between the "REC" and the "Sampler" buttons (Ex. 13), is pressed.

Ex. 13

Each effects unit has two control modes, which can both be fully customized: Single FX Mode and Multi FX mode.

Single FX Mode can be selected by clicking on the Single FX Mode button (Ex. 13.1).

Ex. 13.1

Effects can be selected by clicking on the drop-down menu. Several parameters can then be adjusted by turning the corresponding knobs (Ex. 13.2).

Clicking on the "On" button will switch the effect on or off.

Ex. 13.2

Module 2. Multi FX Mode

Multi FX Mode can be selected by clicking on the Multi FX Mode button (Ex. 13.3).

Pressing the "ON" buttons enables the effect(s), and the rotary knobs will set how much of each effect is heard. Each effect has its own individual drop-down menu onto which effects can be loaded. Up to three effects per FX effects bank can be used, but a single parameter can be adjusted, the effect's depth.

Ex. 13.3

The Beat Multiplier function (Ex. 13.4) is present in both Single FX and Multi FX modes. This function allows the user to shorten or extend the time during which the effect is heard. By default, this time is calculated based on the track's BPM value, but it can be changed to as little as 1/16 of that value, or to as much as eight times that value.

Ex. 13.4

Module 3. Tap Tempo/BPM, Favorite FX Lists, and FX Channel Assign

If a track loaded on the deck assigned to the effects unit has existing BPM information, then this value will automatically appear (Ex. 13.5).

Ex. 13.5

If the track doesn't have BPM information, the word "TAP" will appear where the BPM information should be. It is then possible to manually input this information by steadily tapping this button with your mouse or your trackpad.

It is possible to create a "Favorite FX" list by clicking on the "FX" tab in the Settings panel (Ex. 13.6), choosing favorite effects, and checking the "Use Favorite FX List" box. Only the effects selected in the "Favorite FX" list will appear in the Effect units' drop-down menus.

When Serato DJ Pro is launched, the left effect unit is routed to the left virtual deck, and the right effect unit is routed to the right virtual deck. However, both effect units can be assigned to the same virtual deck. Either effect unit can also be routed to any output channel, or to the Master Output (Ex. 13.7).

In some cases, depending on the hardware used, the effect units can be assigned to an Auxiliary channel or to a Master channel when using hardware supporting four decks, such as high-end controllers.

Ex. 13.6

Ex. 13.7

Unit Fourteen: Music File Management

Description

In this unit, you will learn about creating Crates, Subcrates, and Smart Crates. You will also learn about the History window and how to use the Prepare window. Finally, you will learn about Playlists.

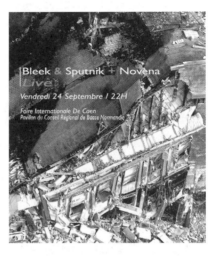

Upon completion of this unit, you should be able to:

- Organize your music by using Crates, Subcrates, and Smart Crates

- Organize your mixes by using the History and the Prepare windows

- Create Playlists

Module 1. Crates, Subcrates, and Smart Crates

Crates

In addition to loading iTunes libraries and playlists, Serato DJ Pro organizes music files into crates so the user can easily access various collections of tracks. The software offers the creation of an unlimited number of crates, and the same track can be placed in several crates.

Adding crates is easy. Just press the "ADD NEW CRATE" button located below the left virtual deck. The user can rename the crate by double-clicking on the crate name once it is created. It is useful to check the "Protect Library" option under the "Library + Display" tab in the Setup window. This will prevent accidental modification or deletion of crates. Accidentally deleted crates can be retrieved from the Trash.

Subcrates

Crates can be dragged and dropped inside another Crate and it will become a Subcrate of the Crate it is dragged into. If a Crate is dragged to the left of the Crate panel, it will remain on top of the crate list. If it is dragged to the right, it will automatically become a Subcrate of the first crate on the list.

Smart Crates

To create a Smart Crate, press the "ADD SMART CRATE" button immediately to the right of the "ADD CRATE" button. Smart Crates organize tracks by adding them based  on rules defined by the user. When adding a Smart Crate, a drop-down menu will appear and the user can select which criteria will be applied to add tracks to the Smart Crate.

Checking the "Live Update" box at the bottom left of the Smart Crate Rules drop-down menu (Ex. 14) automatically updates the track whenever a tag verifying one of the defined rules is added to a track in the library. When the "Live Update" box is left unchecked, the Smart Crate will only update and add tracks verifying one of the rules when the user presses the "REFRESH" icon to the right of the Smart Crate name on the crate list. This "REFRESH" icon only appears when the "Live Update" box is left unchecked.

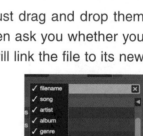

Ex. 14

To edit Smart Crate criteria after having saved it, select it in the left column and press the "EDIT" button that will appear to the right of the "ADD SMART CRATE" button.

Checking the "Match All the Following Rules" ensures that the list follows all the rules described in the drop-down menu. Leaving this option unchecked will add any track that follows any of the rules to the Smart Crate.

Copying, Deleting, and Moving Crates

Crates and files inside them can be deleted by pressing the CTRL + "DEL" shortcut, as long as the "PROTECT LIBRARY" option is unchecked in the "Library+Display" tab of the setup screen.

Ex. 14.1

Copying Crates and files to a new location or a different drive is possible: Just drag and drop them to the new location within the "Files" window. A pop-up window (Ex. 14.1) will then ask you whether you would like to remove the original references from the library. Checking this box will link the file to its new location; leaving it unchecked will keep linking the file to its current location.

Module 2. Searching and Organizing Files

Searching

Clicking on the left of the Search box, which is on the right side of the main display, will open a drop-down menu (Ex. 14.2) with criteria the user can check to restrict the search fields. The user can then type the first few letters of his/her search, and Serato DJ Pro will immediately display the search results. Pressing the CTRL + "F" keyboard shortcut will automatically place the cursor in the Search box and perform a search on the user's entire library, regardless of the Crate or Playlist the user might be browsing at that moment.

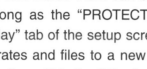

Ex. 14.2

Organizing Files

Similarly, clicking on the arrow located at top of the library on the right will open a drop-down menu (Ex. 14.3) that will indicate the criteria the user can select to display the tracks contained in the library. The user can then click on one of the column headers to organize the library based on that column. Just like in iTunes, drag column headers to the left or the right to move them. Clicking and dragging the column boundaries can also resize columns.

Ex. 14.3

Song Browser

Clicking on the "Browse" button will turn on the Song Browser (Ex. 14.4). Songs can then be organized based on

Ex. 14.4

four criteria: "Genre," BPM," "Artist," and "Album."

Module 3. History Window and Prepare Window

History Window

Pressing the "History" button will open up a window (Ex. 14.5) showing all the Serato DJ Pro sessions that have been performed on

Ex. 14.5

the user's machine. Each session is organized by date and time, and shows by default the name of the track, the name of the artist, the start time of the track, the end time of the track, the track playtime, and a "Notes" field as well as the deck on which the track was played. These fields can be edited by pressing the arrow immediately below the Search field.

Start, End, Save, and Export Sessions

While having the History window open, it is possible to Start, End, Save, and Export Sessions using the buttons below the

Session list. Inserting a track that wasn't actually played in Serato DJ Pro (such as actual CDs or real vinyl) is also possible by pressing the "Insert Track" button. This will cause a new track to be added at the end of the Session track list. This new track can then be double-clicked to be edited.

Sessions can be exported in several popular formats, such as "Serato Playlist," .txt (text), .csv ("Comma Separated Values"), and .m3u (Playlist file format).

It is possible to create a new Crate with tracks played during a specific session: just select the session and drag it to the "New Crate" icon.

Unplayed Tracks

It is possible to display tracks that were auditioned but not played by pressing the "Show Unplayed Tracks" button. These tracks will be displayed as grey and be manually marked as "played" or "unplayed" by pressing the "Mark as Unplayed" button. Pressing the "Clear" button will reset the list of tracks and revert the colors of all the tracks back to white.

Prepare Window

The "Prepare" window (Ex. 14.6) allows the user to set tracks aside that could possibly be played during a set. Entire crates or individual tracks can be

Ex. 14.6

dragged into the Prepare window. These tracks will disappear once they have been played or when the user exits Serato DJ Pro.

The keyboard shortcut for adding tracks to the Prepare window is CTRL + "P." As with the History window, dragging all the Prepare window's tracks to the "Add New Crate" button will create a new crate.

Module 4. Additional File Management Options

Uploading Sessions Online

It is possible for the user to upload History sessions to his/her Serato.com profile once a session is complete. To achieve this, the "Enable Serato Playlists" box must first be checked in the Playlists option under the "Expansions Packs" tab in the Setup menu (Ex. 14.7).

The user can then select a Session in the History window, select the "Serato Playlists" in the Format drop-down menu, then

Ex. 14.7

press the "Export" button. The user will then be taken to Serato.com where the playlist can be reviewed and edited before being posted online.

These playlists can also be uploaded in real time by using the Live Playlist feature. This way, the user can display online what he/she is playing in real time. This is achieved by first checking "Enable Live Playlists" in the Playlists option under the "Expansion Packs" tab in the Setup menu, and then by pressing the "START LIVE PLAYLIST" button in the History window.

Editing Track Information

Some track information (also known as ID3 tags) can be edited within Serato DJ Pro by double-clicking song fields within the main Library. Please note that file names, lengths, sizes, bit rates, and sampling rates cannot be edited. The user will not be able to edit ID3 information if the "Protect Library" box is checked under the "Library+Display" tab in the Setting menu. Once a track to be edited is selected, the keyboard shortcut to quickly edit its file information is CTRL + "e."

File Status Icons

 Various icons displayed in the first column within the Main library show the status of each file: Files displaying this icon have been imported from iTunes and can be played.

 Files displaying these icons are corrupt. It is recommended to re-encode these files.

 Files displaying these icons cannot be found. They usually have been moved and renamed.

 These files are Read Only files and cannot be modified.

File Management Window

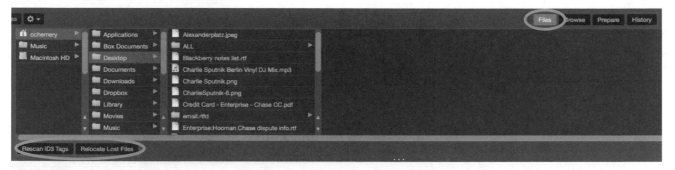

Ex. 14.8

Clicking on the "Files" button (Ex. 14.8) will open up a window showing your computer's files and folders. Below this window, the "Rescan ID3 Tags" function helps the user identify all the files that Serato DJ Pro cannot find. As these files have likely been moved or renamed, this function allows the user to view them in one place. If the software cannot locate files, it will show them in red with a question mark to the left of the track name. It is also possible to drag files one by one to the "Rescan ID3 Tags" button.

Once the missing files have been identified, it is possible to link to their new location by pressing the "Relocate Lost Files" button. The software will look for the files on all of the user's drives. When the files have been found, the library will be updated with the files' new locations. Files and folders can also be "dropped" onto the "Relocate Lost Files" button for individual file relocation.

Serato DJ Pro Backup

Upon exiting the software, if the library has not been backed up in over a week, the user will be asked whether he/she would like to back up his/her Serato DJ Pro Library. Choosing to go forward to backing up the library will either create a new DJ Backup folder, if there isn't any yet, or overwrite the previous backup folder. This folder contains the Library database and the Crate information, but it doesn't contain the actual music files. These must be backed up separately.

Unit Fifteen: Recording

15

Description

In this unit, you will learn about the recording options offered by Serato DJ Pro. These include recording outside sources as well as the ability to instantly stream those sources to one of the Virtual Decks.

Upon completion of this unit, you should be able to:

- Record outside sources into Serato DJ Pro

- Sample from vinyl records

- Record your DJ mixes via a variety of Serato hardware

Module 1. Recording

Clicking on the "REC" button immediately to the left of the "FX" button (Ex. 15) opens up the Recording panel (Ex. 15.1).

Ex. 15

Ex. 15.1

Once this panel is open, select the input source from the drop-down menu. Serato DJ Pro can record one source of stereo signal at a time. In the example on the left, the source can be routed via stereo inputs on the Serato box on channels 1, 2, or 3. Various numbers of channels are available depending on the hardware used (see next chapter).

Press the red "REC" button located between the Recording level meter and the Elapsed Recording Time display. The "REC" button will turn red, and the "TIME ELAPSED" will show the elapsed recording time. The keyboard shortcut for recording is SHIFT + "N."

Press the "REC" button again to stop the recording. Type the name of the new recording in the Filename field and press the "Save" icon immediately to the right of the Filename field.

A new recording file will be created once the length of the recording exceeds three hours at 16-bit depth or 1h50m at 24-bit depth.

It is possible to load a recording onto one the decks without saving it first by using the shortcut SHIFT + left arrow for the Left deck and SHIFT + right arrow for the Right deck.

Module 2. Adjusting Record Settings and Saving Recordings

Adjusting Record Settings

Before starting a new recording, it is a good idea to first play the source audio and set the ideal gain level of the incoming audio by adjusting the Gain control knob located between the Record Location button and the Recording level meter. Ideal level for this setting is for the audio to be as loud as possible within reaching the red LED.

It is possible to adjust the depth of the recordings by selecting either 16-bit or 24-bit depth on the "RECORDING" panel under the

"DJ Preferences" tab in the Setup screen. The file format can also be set to WAV. Serato DJ Pro will also automatically determine whether the input level is Phono or Line level.

It is possible to change the location where recordings are saved when saving them. By default, they are set to be saved in the following folders: "Users > Music >_Serato_/Recording" on a Mac and "MyDocuments > My Music >_Serato_> Recording" on a PC.

Module 3. Recording Options Depending on Hardware

Serato DJ Pro offers a variety of options for recording DJ sets depending on the hardware used:

Recording with a Rane SL-2

The SL-2 only has L and R outputs, so you will need to record your set into a third-party software, such as Audacity. Connect a stereo RCA to a 1/8-inch "Y" cable between the RCA Master outputs of your mixer and the "mini jack" (1/8-inch) input of your computer. Play a track on Serato DJ Pro and record-enable your third-party software. Adjust recording input levels accordingly on third-party software to ensure no clipping occurs, press "Record," and start your mix.

Ex. 15.2

Recording with a Rane SL-3

Connect an RCA cable from your mixer's output to the AUX inputs of the SL-3. Open the "REC" tab in Serato DJ Pro and set the input to "Channel 3." Set the AUX switch on the SL-3 to "Line" level. Once you have adjusted the levels to make sure no clipping occurs, press "REC" in Serato DJ Pro and start your mix. Once finished, enter a name for your mix and save it in Serato DJ.

Ex. 15.3

Recording with a Rane SL-4

Connect an RCA cable from your mixer's output to the AUX inputs of the SL-4. Open the "REC" tab in Serato DJ Pro and set the input to "AUX." Set the AUX switch on the SL-4 to "Line" level. Once you have adjusted the recording levels, press "REC" in Serato DJ Pro and start your mix. Once finished, enter a name for your mix and save it in Serato DJ Pro.

Ex. 15.4

Recording with a Serato DJ-Enabled Mixer

Ex. 15.5

The output signal from Serato DJ-enabled mixers returns to Serato DJ Pro via the USB cable, so no RCA cable is needed to record a DJ set. Open the "REC" tab in Serato DJ Pro and set the input to "MIX." Once you have adjusted the recording levels to make sure no clipping occurs, press "REC" in Serato DJ Pro and start your mix. Once finished, enter a name for your mix and save it in Serato DJ Pro.

Recording with a Controller

Open the "REC" tab in Serato DJ Pro and set the input to "MIX." Once you have adjusted the recording levels to make sure no clipping occurs, press "REC" in Serato DJ Pro and start your mix. Once finished, enter a name for your mix and save it in Serato DJ Pro.

Ex. 15.6

A Appendix A: Charlie's Tips, Tricks, and Advice

Description

In this appendix, you will learn about DJ tips and tricks and receive valuable advice that will help you make the right decisions and avoid making mistakes.

Upon completion of this section, you should be able to:

- Make appropriate creative, technical, and promotional decisions and avoid rookie mistakes
- Make wise business decisions and solidify business relationships

Module 1. Creative Tips

Practice, Practice, Practice

Although pre-planning an entire set is not recommended, finding tracks that work well together takes preparation. Seasoned DJs have all spent countless hours perfecting their playlists and know exactly which tracks work well together and when to play them. Making different types of playlists for different gigs always works a lot better than having a vague idea of what you are going to play.

Planning Three Records At a Time

Building sets of three records that go along well together allows your set to be smoothly organized from mellow to harder and slow to fast. Having about fifty to sixty tracks ready per hour of set will give you options to go in several directions, since you are only likely to play about twenty tracks per hour. You will be able to remain spontaneous while never getting caught off guard.

Flexibility Is Key

Although you should never feel obliged to take requests, especially for tracks you don't like, pleasing that key individual and/or playing more than one specific style might go a long way to ensure future opportunities. Having a large selection to choose from will ensure that you are ready to face different types of crowds.

Know Your Crowd and Your Time Slot

It is crucially important for an opening DJ to properly pace the night. Carefully constructing your set and building it progressively will always work better than trying to blow up the dance floor too early. Most nights are constructed around an energy arc matching the time and the frame of mind of the crowd. Knowing people's frame of mind during your time slot is essential to deliver a successful set. Figuring out the appropriate music to play also depends on factors such as the size of the room and the number of attendees. DJing is not about playing all your favorite music all of the time; it's about connecting with people.

Pushing and Pulling

Giving the crowd enough energy to get everyone excited and dancing is important, but you must be careful not to give it all up too soon. The slower you give the crowd what they want, the longer you will be able to keep them with you, begging for more.

Watch Your Volume

When your music is connecting with the crowd and people are dancing, it is sometimes tempting to push the master volume in the red. The problem with this is that there is a real risk for the music to become distorted, which can seriously affect the vibe of the night. It's important for a DJ to take the headphones off once in awhile to make sure the level in the room isn't too loud or distorted.

Use Your EQs Wisely

As a general rule, EQs should be left at 12 noon, unless a specific adjustment needs to be made on a particular song. Never forget to return the setting to the default noon position once the song is over, for the next song might need a completely different EQ setting or no adjustment at all. Cutting signal instead of boosting it achieves the exact same goal and prevents distortion, even if this requires boosting the gain up a little. For example, don't boost the bass, just cut some mids and highs, and turn the gain up a bit. Also remember that bass frequencies get "muddy" very quickly when played together, so make sure to only introduce one bass source at a time, especially sub-basses.

Effects Are Best Used Sparingly

It is always best to use EQs and levels to create dynamics than relying on effects too much. By now, crowds are familiar with stutter effects, filters, delays, and echos. Best to keep those special by using them sparingly.

Should You Accept a Gig If the Style of Music Required Is Not Your Style of Choice?

Aside from asking yourself if you will have fun playing different music than what you are accustomed to, make sure the challenge of being ready for mixing in a different style is worth the trouble. Even if the fee offered is substantially higher than what you would normally accept (and it should be, in this case), the time and effort involved in getting prepared should definitely be taken into consideration.

First of all, you should set aside plenty of research time to gather a sufficient amount of music, listen to every track at least once, and to practice mixing these new tracks. The ability to mix tracks in a certain genre doesn't necessarily translate to other genres, so practicing transitions is essential.

If the crowd you will be playing to is accustomed to a certain genre and expecting certain tracks, make sure you have all said tracks. If you have time, going out to a few events before your show will let you evaluate the dance-floor appeal of certain tracks. Also, don't let yourself be fooled by DJ lists or charts, because the opinion of other DJs doesn't necessarily reflect what the crowds like.

Refusing to play a gig because there isn't enough time to prepare for it might actually be a blessing in disguise: A promoter is more likely to consider you for future gigs if you refused to play a particular party you know you cannot play, provided you tell that promoter your style of choice. There is nothing worse than to do a poor job at a gig you were not prepared for, as the same promoter will make sure to tell his fellow promoters never to hire you. Once your name is associated with a bad performance, it's really difficult to break that stigma. Don't ever take the risk of ruining your name for a fistful of dollars.

Although it's always good to broaden your horizons to avoid getting pigeonholed in a specific genre, practicing at home is essential before accepting gigs in new genres.

Module 2. Promotional and Technical Tips

Be Visible Online

In addition to your Facebook and Twitter accounts, make sure you are building a fan base by signing up for SoundCloud and Mixcloud accounts. These are among the best resources to get your DJ mixes out there. Broadcast your mixing to the world by playing online radio shows. Get support from key tastemakers of your local scene by promoting their tracks in your sets as well as their events.

Create a Following

Immersing yourself in the scene is the first step, as promoters go out all the time and notice who is out as well. Connecting with promoters without asking them when they will book you next is also a good move, especially on a "dead" night with no big name. Promoters always appreciate the support. Building an email list and/or a Twitter following is also important, and your ability to promote by contacting fans is going to be a great asset. Collaborating and teaming up with other DJs with similar sounds and interests will multiply your chances of succeeding. Offering to pass out flyers or forwarding party announcements goes a long way to show promoters you are on their team, even before they book you.

Once You've Been Booked

Making sure your party is a success by promoting heavily is a key factor to show club owners and promoters that you are serious. Collecting emails will increase your reach as well. Making sure you remain professional during your party by not drinking excessively will also surely be noticed.

Protecting Your Gear

If you use a digital setup, bringing a clone of your hard drive will save your life if the one you regularly use refuses to boot up. Putting your sets on the cloud (using services such as Dropbox, Amazon Cloud Drive, Google Music, etc.) will make your tracks available for re-download if your hard drive were to ever fail.

Using protective bags, cases, or pouches is a necessity, especially if you start to play out a lot. Unfortunately, the most dangerous places for your gear are precisely the ones you are performing in—the clubs.

Checklists

Preparing checklists for gigs is a great idea, especially when you are required to bring most of the equipment (turntables, speakers, cables, etc.). Making sure your list is complete before the gig is as important as ensuring nothing is missing once you're done playing.

Be Prepared for Unexpected Situations

A DJ can never expect which piece of equipment might start malfunctioning during a set. For this reason, it's always a good idea to bring music in different formats and coming from different sources. Ideally, a DJ should have some vinyl records, CDs, a backup USB key, and an MP3 player in case everything else fails.

Be Selective About Who You Allow in Your DJ Booth

Drinks are quickly spilled, and electronics and liquids don't go together well. To shield yourself from accidents (as well as from excessive music requests), ask the club owner if a security guard can be posted by the booth. If this is not possible, you will need to enforce a strict no-access policy. This will also help you focus on your mixing and prevent you from being distracted.

Use Gaffer's Tape

Taping down your controllers, laptops, and hard drives will prevent them from falling about especially if your booth is overrun, which sometimes happens. Also, it is crucial to keep your soundcard's USB connection firmly in place so it doesn't get pulled out accidentally.

Use Earplugs

DJs get exposed to excessive levels of music on a regular basis, so a pair of earplugs is best kept handy at all times.

Leave Your Gear in a Secure Place Once You've Played Your Set

The DJ booth is not a safe place to leave your expensive gear. Taking your gear with you can be a bit bothersome, especially if your car is parked far away, so the best bet is to ask for the club owner or promoter to lock up your equipment for you.

Module 3. Business Tips

DJ Insurance

Having good insurance for your gear is always a good idea if you play in places where your gear might be damaged or stolen, meaning most places. Most major insurance companies offer music equipment insurance.

Contracts and Riders

Although negotiating a DJ rider may seem like a tricky situation at first, it will protect you in case anything goes wrong.

The **basic** contract is specific to the show and typically identifies the parties concerned and covers the date, time, fee, and any guarantees based on attendance, bar sales, etc. A radius clause limiting performances in the same geographic area before and after the show might also be included in the agreement.

It should look like this:

EVENT DETAILS

Date of Show:	January 5, 2018
Time of Show:	9PM–2AM
Sound Check:	8PM
Total Artist Fee:	$1,000

ARTIST PROVISIONS

Flight:	N/A
Hotel:	N/A
Transportation:	N/A
Meals:	N/A

PAYMENT SCHEDULE

Deposit:	$500 (USD) due within one week upon receipt of contract
Balance:	$500 (USD) due on date of performance

The **rider** covers the equipment, transportation, and cancellation policies, comps, and catering preferences. Food, drinks, transportation, lodging, and per diems should also be included, if applicable. The rider should also specify that you are included in all promotional efforts linked to the event.

In the event that the basic contract also mentions an item also covered on the rider, it is important to protect yourself in case the terms contradict themselves in any way. To achieve this, make sure the rider mentions the following:

"In the event a discrepancy should arise between the provisions of this Rider and the provisions of any other part of this Agreement, the provisions of this Rider shall apply."

Often times, the basic contract is provided by the club and the rider is provided by the DJ.

Cancellation Policy

It is important that the cancellation policy doesn't make you responsible for occurrences beyond your control, such as grave illness or a car accident on the way to the show. The policy also usually deals with voluntary cancellation when either you or the club decides to terminate the contract before the performance.

Payment

The ideal situation is when 50% of the fee is due upon signing and the remaining 50% is due within an hour after the set is completed. The initial 50% should be non-refundable except if you voluntarily cancel the show. If the club doesn't agree to pay any fee upfront, then you can try to insert language stating that the club owes 50% of the fee if they cancel within 48 hours of the show, and/or the entire fee if they cancel within 24 hours.

Equipment

Make sure to mention your ideal setup in your rider, including the make and model of each piece of equipment. Do not bring your own equipment if you can avoid it (mixers, etc.): not only will you not have to carry heavy boxes, but you also won't risk having it damaged. Any equipment that you must bring should be covered by the club's insurance policy.

Appendix B: Charlie's Example Entry Level Setup

B

Description

In this appendix, you will learn about the entry-level DJ setup that Charlie uses within the accompanying videos.

Upon completion of this section, you should be able to:

- Understand the equipment that Charlie utilized within the video lessons

- Comprehend how each item is connected to the main DJ mixer

Module 1. Pioneer DJM-350 Mixer

Overview

The Pioneer DJM-350 is a two-channel mixer featuring four dedicated effects as well as an isolated 3-band equalizer. A front USB port allows for mixes to be recorded and stored onto USB storage devices. The unit also provides digital conversion for higher quality sound.

Ins and Outs

The mixer features two CD/Line RCA inputs, two Phono RCA inputs, one microphone (1/4 inch) input, and one AUX RCA input. There are two Master RCA outputs.

Features

The mixer features 48 kHz/24-bit digital signal processing, cross fader start control, cross fader curve adjustment, and very sturdy faders and rotaries. The Master effects section is controlled by a single rotary level/depth knob. Four large on/off buttons switch between Gate/Jet (Flanger/Phaser), Crush, and Filter effects. However, these effects cannot be combined and are Master effects only, meaning they cannot be assigned to individual channels or to the Mic/Aux inputs. Also, they can only be applied one at a time, so no layering is possible.

The Mixer has an AUX RCA input, which can serve as another channel when mixing, making the playback of any external line input (such as a CD or MP3 player) possible. However, the Mixer doesn't allow for the Mic and the AUX inputs to be used simultaneously: the toggle switch above the channel has to be selected to one or the other.

One of the mixer's most notable features is its ability to record mixes in WAV format by inserting a USB stick and just pressing the "record" button. Pressing the "record" button while the track is already recording can set a track marker. Once track markers are set, easy preview navigation is possible by using the "Preview," "Next," and "Previous" buttons. This feature makes the creation of gapless mix CDs possible, while retaining track-skipping ability.

Each channel features a 3-band isolator EQ as well as its own gain control knob. Each EQ frequency (Low, Mids, and Highs) can be completely turned off by turning the knobs all the way down.

The mixer's Cue section is located on the lower left corner of the mixer and features a headphone volume control knob and a Mix/Cue knob for monitoring. CH-1 and CH-2 buttons are used to listen to corresponding channels via headphones.

The unit also comes with the Pioneer RekordBox software, which allows preparing and managing music files for DJ sets.

Conclusion

The Pioneer DJM-350 mixer offers a very rugged and affordable club-quality solution. Pros include a solid all-steel chassis; high-quality faders, switches, knobs, and buttons; very high sound quality and accurate EQ; USB onboard direct recording and playback; and onboard effects. The cons include the absence of Unbalanced and/or XLR outputs, the impossibility to layer effects, and the impossibility to use the Mic and AUX inputs simultaneously.

Module 2. Pioneer CDJ-350 CD Turntable

Overview

The Pioneer CDJ-350 is a digital media player that can play audio CDs and MP3 CDs, as well as digital files stored on USB storage devices. The unit is also a MIDI-HID controller. It also features a built-in soundcard that can be used with any mixing software. The media player also includes Pioneer's proprietary music management software, Rekordbox, which makes it possible to manage music files on a computer for quick selection when played back on compatible Pioneer players.

Ins and Outs

Two audio RCA outs and two USB ports—one (A-Type) on top of the unit to connect USB storage units, and one (B-Type) at the back of the unit to control external DJ software.

Features

The unit is compatible with a number of media formats, including MP3, WAV, AIFF, and AAC. CD-R/RW discs can be played as well as conventional CDs. BPM Lock is one of the main features of the CDJ-350. This feature relies on the machine's ability to precisely analyze BPMs. By holding down the BPM Lock button, the user can select a master tempo for the mix, ensuring that every track that is loaded from any media is automatically set to that tempo. Although this feature greatly eases the beat matching process, it doesn't provide automatic synchronization between decks as software such as Ableton Live or Traktor do.

The onscreen beat indicator ("BEAT DISPLAY") shows a basic view of a bar moving through each beat, making scratching on a beat or bar-match mixing much easier.

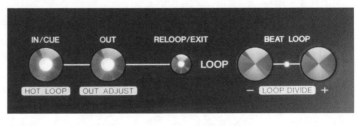

Loop In/Cue and Loop Out define loop starting and ending points. The loop will play until the Reloop/Exit button is pressed. Pressing this button again will replay the last loop. While the loop is playing, pressing the Hot Loop button will start the loop again from the beginning.

Loop lengths can be divided or doubled by pressing the "-" or "+" buttons. This function also works with homemade loops. Loop length can be divided until the loop is only one frame long, and can be doubled in length.

The player also has a vibration-resistance feature, four levels of tempo settings (±6%, ±10%, ±16%, and WIDE), and a Resume function that enables users to remove a disc and resume playback at the same spot when the disc is reloaded.

Touch Sensitive Jog Dial

The Jog Dial's outer upstanding ring is used to make pitch corrections or pitch bends. Gently rotating the dial clockwise without pressing the top part of the dial will pitch the track up, whereas an anti-clockwise rotation will result in a pitch decrease slowing the track down. When the player is in Vinyl mode, only the outer ring of the jog wheel is activated. Pressing the black top of the dial will pause playing and enable vinyl-like scratching.

Basic Connection Setup

When connected to a Pioneer mixer using the control cord, operations such as starting playback on this unit can be controlled using the mixer's fader. Sliding the fader back will return the track to the cue point previously selected on the unit. The fader start function can only be used when connected to a Pioneer DJ mixer.

Relay Connection Setup

When connected directly to each other via the control cord, Relay playback between two CDJ-350 units is possible by switching on Auto Cue: when a track ends on the first player, the other player will start from the Auto Cue point onwards. The next track is cued on the second player, waiting for the first track's "End" signal.

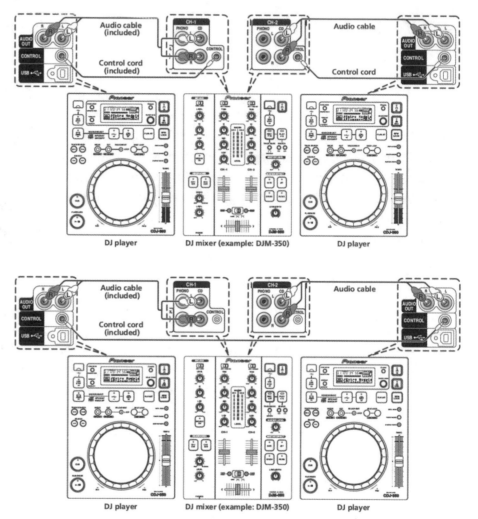

DJ player   DJ mixer (example: DJM-350)   DJ player

If the Playlist button is pressed when a track is playing, the track is added to a playlist, stored on the USB medium. These playlists can be imported into Rekordbox for future use.

Conclusion

USB connectivity and the Rekordbox software make this media player future-proof by guaranteeing compatibility with ever-improving software solutions. However, the player remains compatible with a wide variety of existing formats. The pros include sturdiness, reliability, USB connectivity, a BPM lock feature (which greatly eases the beat matching process and is therefore ideal for beginners), and a useful onscreen beat indicator. Cons include non-weighted jog wheels that feel a bit flimsy and the lack of any effects.

Module 3. Numark TTX-USB Vinyl Turntable

Overview

The TTX-USB has a lot of features fitting the modern DJ's needs. In addition to an interchangeable tone arm system that adapts to any DJ style, the turntable has a silicone base that absorbs vibrations and dampens low-end feedback. The unit also features an illuminated display, a built-in BPM counter, and a built-in USB connector for professional grade vinyl-to-digital transfers. The bundled EZ Vinyl Converter software converts vinyl tracks directly to iTunes.

Ins and Outs

The unit's connection panel features a USB connection for ultra-quick conversion of vinyl to digital media, a selectable phone/line level output, and a gain knob as well as a voltage selector making the unit usable anywhere in the world.

Features

The neon blue circular display shows pitch, platter speed, and BPM, as well as the start and brake settings when adjusting. The

unit has two large start/stop buttons in the corners, making the deck ideally accessible to both left- and right-handed users. Right above the buttons sits a start and brake dial giving a 0–9 second adjustment range.

The pitch slider and speed controls can be unscrewed and swapped around, so that the pitch won't be obstructed by the tone arm, a useful trick for battle DJs. The display will detect which configuration is used and rotate automatically.

The tone arm assembly has a fully lockable height adjustment and anti-skate control. The particularity of the unit is that it allows easy swapping between "S" and "Straight" arms. The "S" arm is a bit longer, and therefore a tad heavier, so it comes with a small counterbalance to be screwed into the end of the tone arm.

The unit can be adjusted to 33, 45, and 78 RPM, which makes it a great archiving tool for ancient 78 RPM records. The pitch range can be set to 8, 10, 25, and 50%. The TTX also comes with a side strobe that switches depending on the platter speed selected. A truly impressive feature for a vinyl deck is the Key Lock feature: adjusting speed without affecting pitch is possible, making harmonic mixing a lot easier. This feature is only available to the line output, however.

Conclusion

This turntable is extremely sturdy and solid and can withstand years of heavy use. Its USB connectivity makes it ideal for archiving rare vinyl directly to iTunes, and the adjustable gain control is very useful. The interchangeability of the arms suits every kind of DJ, and the possibility of swapping pitch sliders and speed controls makes the unit even more customizable. The outputs located below the unit can make it challenging to quickly connect and disconnect, though, but overall, this unit is of very high quality.

Appendix C: Charlie's Rhythms, Meter, and Pulse

Description

In this unit you will learn about the symbols and components involved with reading rhythmic notation.

Upon completion of this section, you should be able to:

- Identify the staff, whole notes, half notes, and quarter notes, along with corresponding rests, measures, time signatures, BPM, and repeat signs

- Understand the rhythmic values of whole notes, half notes, and quarter notes, along with the corresponding rests

- Understand the Breakbeat and its function in popular music

- Apply these rhythmic ideas to beat matching and feeling music, while DJing or listening to music

Module 1. Basic Notation Components

For a professional DJ, reading detailed musical notation is not necessary. However, the ability to feel musical pulses such as whole, half, and quarter notes can save a lot of time. For example, beat matching or combining complex songs or passages by ear can be very time-consuming. If one is able to feel music in its most basic subdivisions, then it can help speed up the learning process and the overall workflow. In this section, you will be shown the tools needed to feel musical pulses. Let's take a look at each building block below.

This unit starts with the most basic building blocks of musical rhythm. This is the foundation from which all music builds upon. An understanding of the symbols and concepts below is the first step to comprehending musical subdivision.

The Staff

The staff is an arrangement of five parallel lines, and the four spaces between them. Both lines and spaces can represent musical notes (or pitches).

Ex. C.1

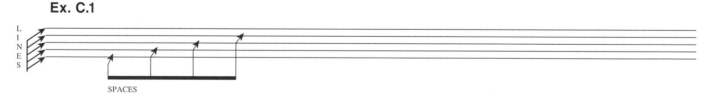

LINES

SPACES

Structural Elements

Bar Lines

The staff is divided into measures by using single bar lines. As you will see in Ex. C.2 below, these lines also correspond with (and reset) the meter.

Ex. C.2

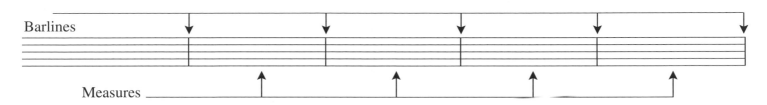

There are also other types of bar lines, such as:

The **double bar line** separates sections of music within a single piece of music. This is a visual aid for the performer to keep his or her place while reading the music.

A **final bar line** is placed at the end of a piece of music to confirm the ending.

Ex. C.3

Repeat Signs

A **repeat sign**, notated below with the bracketed bar lines and the two vertical dots, is the symbol that indicates a section should be repeated.

Ex. C.4

Repeat the section between these two symbols.

Meter

Meter can be thought of as the pulse, the heartbeat of a piece of music. All music has momentum—a forward moving pulse that is counted in beats. Meter is measured in groups of beats with the most common being groups of two, three, or four beats. For example:

Meter	Music
2 Beats	Country, Marches, Polka
3 Beats	Waltz
4 Beats	Pop, Rock, R&B

Counting Beats

Once the meter of a piece of music is deciphered, a counting system is then put in place that represents the passing of each measure. For example:

Ex. C.5

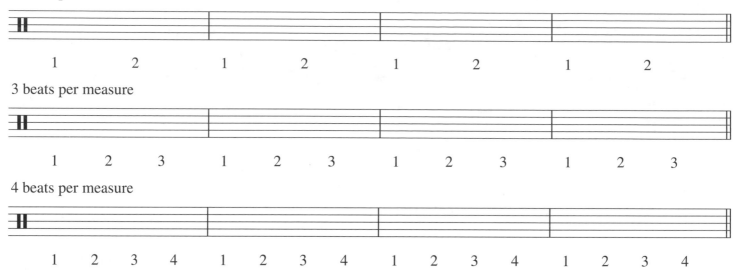

Time Signature

A **time signature** indicates the meter of a piece of music and the corresponding note value used within its notation. Placed to the right of the clef, the time signature is displayed as a stack of two numbers. The top number indicates how many beats there are in each measure. The bottom number displays the value of each beat. Values will be explained in the next chapter.

For example:

Ex. C.6

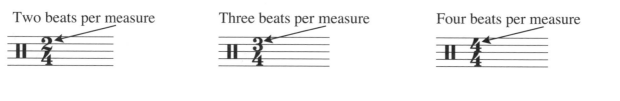

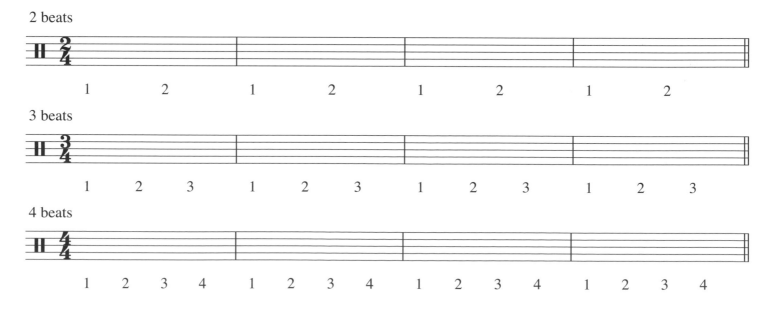

C = Common Time Symbol

The most common meter in music is 4/4. For clarity purposes, the "4/4" time signature may be replaced simply by the letter C. For example:

Ex. C.7

Beats Per Minute (BPM)

BPM represents the pace (or tempo) of music measured by the number of beats occurring in 60 seconds (or one minute). Commonly, the BPM is indicated at the top of a piece of music. For instance, the following piece of music should be played at 120 bpm, which can be notated two ways (i.e., as BPM or with a quarter note equaling the BPM):

Ex. C.8

or

120 bpm

Module 2. Rhythmic Values

Within a 4/4 time signature (four beats per measure) there are three main note values: whole note, half note, and quarter note.

Whole Note

A whole note is equal to four beats (i.e., a *whole* measure) and is indicated by a hollow oval note head. It is counted as follows:

Ex. C.9

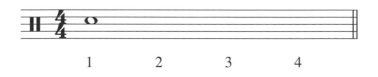

Exercise 1

While counting every beat out loud, clap a whole note on beat 1 of every measure as follows:

Ex. C.10

Half Note

A half note is equal to two beats (*half* of a measure) and is indicated by a hollow oval head with a stem attached. It is counted as follows:

Ex. C.11

Exercise 1

While counting every beat out loud, clap half notes on beats 1 and 3 of every measure as follows:

Ex. C.12

Exercise 2

While counting every beat out loud, clap the whole notes and half notes as follows:

Ex. C.13

Quarter Note

A quarter note is equal to one beat (one *quarter* of a measure) and is indicated by a solid, oval note head with a stem attached. Quarter notes are counted like so:

Ex. C.14

Exercise 1

While counting every beat out loud, clap quarter notes on beats 1 to 4 of every measure as follows:

Ex. C.15

All Together

While counting every beat out loud, clap the whole notes, half notes, and quarter notes as follows:

Ex. C.16

Rhythmic Value Tree: Notes

As you have seen, a whole note is equal to two half notes, which are equal to four quarter notes. For example:

Ex. C.17

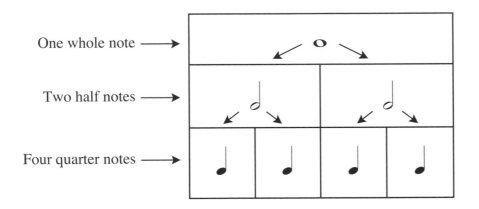

Module 3. The Almighty Drum: Backbeats and More

Listen to any radio hit that uses dance rhythms, drum sets, or loops. What makes this track groove and flow as you are listening to it? Does it feel like a train that cannot be stopped? Is the rhythm so incessant and repetitive that it could groove for days without wavering in its consistency? Are you tapping your foot without even realizing it? If you answered "yes" to any of these questions, then you also realize the exact reason why many artists use these textures in their compositions: they add a relentless, repetitive, and unwavering momentum to a track. As a result, you should not disrupt that momentum: incessant rhythm, train, or foot tapping with inappropriate stutters, sloppy beat matching, or incorrect transitions will detract from (or overshadow) the groove and its inherent drive.

Remember, your listeners are not staring at your gear or the screens located on said gear! You must give them the impression that you and each tune are one huge band of groove. So in order to maintain that illusion, you must blend your stutter fills and subsequent tune choices with the overall repetitive flavor of your current (playing) tune. This not only helps keep the loop/music flowing, but it also makes your mix sound enormous!

Well, what item is present in nearly every popular loop or groove? Answer: the backbeat! So every time you fill, transition, stutter, or beat match, you should include/maintain the backbeat in some shape or form. This important fill trait will help you blend tracks seamlessly and keep people dancing.

With these items in mind, the backbeat is the snare drum that pulses on beats two and four like this:

Ex. C.18

The bass drum is normally played on beats one and three:

Ex. C.19

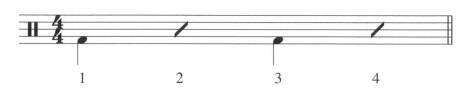

Now let's combine them like this:

Ex. C.20

Video 29

Musicians Institute Press is the official series of instructional publications from Southern California's renowned music school, Musicians Institute. These books, book/audio packages, and videos have been created by MI instructors who are among the world's best and most experienced professional musicians.

KEYBOARD

00695708	Blues Hanon by Peter Deneff	$17.99
00695556	Dictionary of Keyboard Grooves by Gail Johnson – Book/CD	$16.95
00202430	Easy Jazz Hanon by Peter Deneff – Book/Audio	$12.99
00695336	Funk Keyboards – The Complete Method by Gail Johnson – Book/Audio	$16.99
00695936	Hip-Hop Keyboard by Henry Soleh Brewer – Book/CD	$17.95
00695791	Jazz Chord Hanon by Peter Deneff	$17.99
00695554	Jazz Hanon by Peter Deneff	$16.99
00695773	Jazz Piano by Christian Klikovits – Book/CD	$19.99
00695209	Keyboard Voicings by Kevin King	$12.95
00145419	Pop Keyboard Concepts by Christian Klikovits – Book/Audio	$19.99
00695509	Pop Rock Keyboards by Henry Sol-Eh Brewer & David Garfield – Book/CD	$19.95
00695784	Rock Hanon by Peter Deneff	$19.99
00695226	Salsa Hanon by Peter Deneff	$17.99
00695939	Samba Hanon by Peter Deneff	$16.99
00695882	Stride Hanon by Peter Deneff	$17.99

VOICE

00695883	Advanced Vocal Technique by Dena Murray and Tita Hutchison – Book/Audio	$19.99
00695262	Harmony Vocals by Mike Campbell & Tracee Lewis – Book/Audio	$19.99
00695626	The Musician's Guide to Recording Vocals by Dallan Beck – Book/CD	$15.99
00695629	Rock Vocals by Coreen Sheehan – Book/CD	$17.99
00695195	Sightsinging by Mike Campbell	$19.99
00695427	Vocal Technique by Dena Murray – Book/Audio	$24.99

GUITAR

00695922	Acoustic Artistry by Evan Hirschelman – Book/CD	$19.99
00695298	Advanced Scale Concepts and Licks for Guitar by Jean Marc Belkadi – Book/CD	$17.99
00217709	All-in-One Guitar Soloing Course by Daniel Gilbert & Beth Marlis	$29.99
00695132	Blues Guitar Soloing by Keith Wyatt – Book/Online Media	$24.99
00695680	Blues/Rock Soloing for Guitar by Robert Calva – Book/Audio	$19.99
00695131	Blues Rhythm Guitar by Keith Wyatt – Book/Audio	$19.99
00696002	Modern Techniques for the Electric Guitarist by Dean Brown – DVD	$29.95
00695664	Chord Progressions for Guitar by Tom Kolb – Book/CD	$17.99
00695855	Chord Tone Soloing by Barrett Tagliarino – Book/Audio	$24.99
00695646	Chord-Melody Guitar by Bruce Buckingham – Book/CD	$19.99
00695171	Classical & Fingerstyle Guitar Techniques by David Oakes – Book/Audio	$17.99
00695806	Classical Themes for Electric Guitar by Jean Marc Belkadi – Book/CD	$15.99
00695661	Country Guitar by Al Bonhomme – Book/Audio	$19.99
00695227	The Diminished Scale for Guitar by Jean Marc Belkadi – Book/CD	$14.99

00695181	Essential Rhythm Guitar by Steve Trovato – Book/CD	$15.99
00695873	Ethnic Rhythms for Electric Guitar by Jean Marc Belkadi – Book/CD	$17.99
00695860	Exotic Scales & Licks for Electric Guitar by Jean Marc Belkadi – Book/CD	$16.95
00695419	Funk Guitar by Ross Bolton – Book/Audio	$15.99
00695134	Guitar Basics by Bruce Buckingham – Book/Audio	$17.99
00695712	Guitar Fretboard Workbook by Barrett Tagliarino	$19.99
00695321	Guitar Hanon by Peter Deneff	$12.99
00695482	The Guitar Lick•tionary by Dave Hill – Book/CD	$19.99
00695190	Guitar Soloing by Daniel Gilbert and Beth Marlis – Book/Audio	$22.99
00695169	Harmonics by Jamie Findlay – Book/CD	$13.99
00695406	Introduction to Jazz Guitar Soloing by Joe Elliott – Book/CD	$19.95
00695291	Jazz Guitar Chord System by Scott Henderson	$12.99
00217711	Jazz Guitar Improvisation by Sid Jacobs – Book/Online Media	$19.99
00217690	Jazz, Rock & Funk Guitar by Dean Brown – Book/Online Media	$19.99
00695361	Jazz-Rock Triad Improvising for Guitar by Jean Marc Belkadi – Book/CD	$15.99
00695379	Latin Guitar by Bruce Buckingham – Book/Audio	$17.99
00696656	Liquid Legato by Allen Hinds – Book/CD	$14.99
00695143	A Modern Approach to Jazz, Rock & Fusion Guitar by Jean Marc Belkadi – Book/CD	$15.99
00695711	Modern Jazz Concepts for Guitar by Sid Jacobs – Book/CD	$16.95
00695682	Modern Rock Rhythm Guitar by Danny Gill – Book/CD	$16.95
00695555	Modes for Guitar by Tom Kolb – Book/Audio	$18.99
00695192	Music Reading for Guitar by David Oakes	$19.99
00695697	Outside Guitar Licks by Jean Marc Belkadi – Book/CD	$16.99
00695962	Power Plucking by Dale Turner – Book/CD	$19.95
00695748	Progressive Tapping Licks by Jean Marc Belkadi – Book/CD	$16.99
00114559	Rhythm Guitar by Bruce Buckingham & Eric Paschal – Book/Audio	$24.99
00695188	Rhythm Guitar by Bruce Buckingham & Eric Paschal – Book	$19.99
00695909	Rhythm Guitar featuring Bruce Buckingham – DVD	$19.95
00110263	Rhythmic Lead Guitar by Barrett Tagliarino – Book/Audio	$19.99
00695144	Rock Lead Basics by Nick Nolan and Danny Gill – Book/Audio	$18.99
00695910	Rock Lead Guitar featuring Danny Gill – Book/CD	$19.95
00695278	Rock Lead Performance by Nick Nolan and Danny Gill – Book/Audio	$17.99
00695146	Rock Lead Techniques by Nick Nolan and Danny Gill – Book/Audio	$16.99
00695977	Shred Guitar by Greg Harrison – Book/CD	$19.99
00139556	Solo Slap Guitar by Jude Gold – Book/Video	$19.99
00695645	Slap & Pop Technique for Guitar by Jean Marc Belkadi – Book/CD	$15.99
00695913	Technique Exercises for Guitar by Jean Marc Belkadi – Book/CD	$15.99
00695340	Texas Blues Guitar by Robert Calva – Book/Audio	$17.99
00695863	Ultimate Guitar Technique by Bill LaFleur – Book/Audio	$22.99

BASS

DRUMS

ALL INSTRUMENTS

RECORDING

HAL•LEONARD®

www.halleonard.com

Prices, contents and availability subject to change without notice.